The Article V Amendatory Constitutional Convention

The Article V Amendatory Constitutional Convention

Keeping the Republic in the Twenty-First Century

Thomas E. Brennan

LEXINGTON BOOKS
Lanham • Boulder • New York • London

Published by Lexington Books
An imprint of The Rowman & Littlefield Publishing Group, Inc.
4501 Forbes Boulevard, Suite 200, Lanham, Maryland 20706
www.rowman.com

Unit A, Whitacre Mews, 26-34 Stannery Street, London SE11 4AB, United Kingdom

British Library Cataloguing in Publication Information Available

Library of Congress Cataloging-in-Publication Data

Brennan, Thomas E., 1929- author.
The Article V amendatory constitutional convention : keeping the republic in the twenty-first century / Thomas E. Brennan.
pages cm.
Includes bibliographical references and index.
ISBN 978-1-4985-0103-3 (cloth) -- ISBN 978-1-4985-0104-0 (electronic)
1. Constitutional conventions--United States. 2. United States. Constitution. Article 5. I. Title.
KF4555.B69 2014
342.7302'4--dc23

2014026209

∞ ™ The paper used in this publication meets the minimum requirements of American National Standard for Information Sciences Permanence of Paper for Printed Library Materials, ANSI/NISO Z39.48-1992.

Printed in the United States of America

Contents

Preface

In 1973, with the help of several judges and lawyers, I founded the Thomas Cooley Law School in Lansing, Michigan. By the early 1980s, Cooley Law School was well established. Still, there was much to do. For one thing, we needed a Law Review. All respectable law schools have law reviews. Making Law Review is the definition of success to many students.

Fortunately, we had a faculty member on board who knew something about starting academic publications. His name was Spencer Abraham, and he later became a United States Senator. When a student at the Harvard Law School, Abraham had founded the *Harvard Journal of Law and Public Policy*. It is still being published and has earned the kind of prestige normally associated with everything at Harvard.

Professor Abraham agreed to take on the job of faculty moderator of our nascent law review. One of his first initiatives was to persuade me to write the inaugural article for the new publication. I had been away from scholarly writing for a long time. While I had authored many opinions on the Supreme Court, they were not of the truly academic genre. And anyway, even opinion writing was then ten years ago.

I did have an interest, however, which got my juices flowing. Cooley had become a truly national law school. At every welcoming luncheon, I would ask the students from each state to stand and be recognized. There were almost always more than forty states represented. Realizing that they were part of a truly national class always bolstered the enthusiasm of the freshmen. Not to mention how satisfying it was for the faculty and the admissions office.

The decade of the 1980s was a special time in the history of the United States. It was the occasion to celebrate the two hundredth anniversary of the establishment of our nation. Cornwallis's surrender at Yorktown, the recognition of American independence, and finally, the adoption of the United States Constitution made the decade of the 1780s worth remembering.

I came up with the idea of holding a convention as contemplated by Article V of the Federal Constitution, and I invited the student bar association to participate. I told them that, if we could enlist students who were actual voting residents of two-thirds of the states, we would convene and consider whatever amendments the students might propose.

I rented a huge tent which enclosed the parking lot next to the administration building on South Grand Avenue. Rented tables and chairs. Had signs made identifying the states. When the day came, more than two hundred student "delegates" showed up. We had a credentials committee which examined the identification of each attendee, and directed them to the table where their state caucus was ensconced.

Phil Prygoski, our outstanding Con Law professor undertook to deliver the keynote address, whereupon I took the microphone and tried to steer the assembly through the process of introducing, debating, and voting on various proposed constitutional amendments.

It was a great exercise. I was especially touched by some of the personal experiences and backgrounds many of them brought to the table. On some issues, they were predictably liberal. On others, surprisingly traditional.

The age and citizenship criteria for election as President were hotly contested, but ultimately not targeted for change.

The mock convention affirmed my determination to focus my law review article on the process of amending the constitution laid out in Article V.

It would be a labor of love. It was before I became addicted to word processing on the computer. I took out my lawyer-like yellow foolscap pad, and across the top of the first page, I wrote the title.

Return to Philadelphia: A case for the calling of an amendatory convention under Article V of the Federal Constitution.

That article led to an invitation to speak at a symposium at Yale University. The occasion was the founding of the Federalist Society. My remarks were titled *The Last Prerogative.* It was a speech about how Article V was intended to empower the states to fix a dysfunctional federal government.

Twenty-five years later, I got a letter from Harvard asking me to update my Yale speech. The letter piqued my curiosity. I went to the world wide web to see what was happening to Article V. I found a plethora of websites, blogs, organizations, and ideas reflecting citizen dissatisfaction with the national government and a crescent interest in Article V as a solution.

My curiosity led me to Bill Walker, a small town journalist from Washington state. Bill and I, along with author Joel Hirshhorn, media producer Byron DeLear, businessman Dennis Murphy, and publisher John De Herrara launched an organization and a website known as Friends of the Article V Convention.

FOAVC has been the premier effort to provide information about Article V. It has gathered evidence of more than 747 state petitions for an Article V convention, as well as a multitude of essays, articles, and blogs about an amendatory convention.

That effort, in turn, led me to establish Convention USA, an actual gathering of American citizens on the Internet for the purpose of proposing amendments. This book is all about that convention. Why it is needed. What it can do. How it can be accomplished.

This, too, has been a labor of love, one I could never have accomplished without the encouragement of family; son Tom and daughter Peggy especially.

My daughter, Marybeth Hicks, herself an accomplished author of three published works, gave me more than encouragement. She gave me candid and professional criticism, and she has nursed me along the path with everything from nitty gritty computer instruction to the nuances of the publishing business.

The gold medal, of course, goes to Pauline Mary Brennan, the beautiful woman who consented to be my bride more than sixty-three years ago. She has tolerated my endless hours at the computer, read and re-read every page and paragraph, and debated, cajoled, critiqued, and censored every sentence.

Making her proud of me and happy to be my wife is what gets me up in the morning.

So many others have helped; proofreaders, devil's advocates, helpful hinters, cheerleaders. Folks like Gene Mosner, Jim Ryan, Ernie Phillips, Jim Bernard, John Scott, Chuck Bassos, Doug McCormick, Ben Prather. It's a long, long list that includes Brian Hill and Justin Race, my two very new and very capable friends at Lexington Books.

To all, my thanks. I hope you like the book, and that the Author of all Law will continue to smile on the efforts of our Founders and on those who strive to keep the Republic they established.

I

The Problem

Chapter One

Congress Shall, But Congress Won't

On Friday, January 24, 1788, the gallery of the Brattle Street Church in Boston was jammed. Below, on the floor, 350 delegates buzzed with conversations and comments. The issue was section 8 of Article I of the Constitution written in Philadelphia and now being considered for ratification by the representatives of the people of Massachusetts.[1]

Section 8 began with words anathema to men who had defied the King, had dumped tea into the harbor, had fought the Red Coats on Bunker Hill:

"The Congress shall have the power to lay and collect taxes, duties, imposts and excises."[2]

Amos Singletary, a crusty old Worcester farmer rose to speak. Did the convention want to hear from those who fought for independence? He was one of them. What would the freedom fighters have thought of this new constitution?[3]

They would have thrown it away, he insisted. The constitution authorizes taxes, duties, imposts—the very things that they had fought against.

The first white male to be born in the town of Sutton, Singletary and his wife Mary had nine children. Unschooled but self-taught, he served as a Justice of the Peace and a member of the state legislature.

Sixty-six years old, erect and weathered, he spoke with a defiance born in battle:

> These lawyers and men of learning, and moneyed men that talk so finely, and gloss over matters so smoothly, to make us poor illiterate people swallow down the pill, expect to get into Congress themselves. They expect to be the managers of this Constitution, and get all the power and all the money into their own hands. And then they will swallow up us little fellows, like the great Leviathan, Mr. President; yes, just as the whale swallowed up Jonah.[4]

Jonathan Smith, of Lanesborough in the Berkshires rose immediately. Young, soft spoken and calm, he nonetheless quieted the room with his first words:

> Mr. President, I am a plain man and I get my living by the plow. I am not used to speak in public, but I beg your leave to say a few words to my brother plow joggers in this house. I have lived in a part of the country where I have known the worth of good government by the want of it. There was a black cloud that rose in the East last winter and spread to the West. . . .[5]

Shay's Rebellion! He was talking about Shay's rebellion! Suddenly the gallery burst into a tumult of shouting and protest. Smith stood silently, his hands at his sides, his face turned, expressionless, toward the Speaker's podium. The crack of the gavel finally brought a measure of calm, and the authoritative voice of Sam Adams asked the convention to let the young man go on in his own way.

Describing the lawless anarchy that was instigated by Daniel Shay and his followers the previous year, Smith asserted that the people were so frightened and distraught that they would have snatched at "anything that looked like a government" even if it might mean installing a tyrant to keep order. Smith continued:

> Now, Mr. President, when I saw this constitution, I found that it was a cure for these disorders. I got a copy of it and I read it over and over. I had been a member of the Convention to form our own state constitution, and had learned something of the checks and balances of power, and I found them all there. I did not go to any lawyer to ask his opinion. We have no lawyer in our town, and we do well enough without. I formed my own opinion and I was pleased with this Constitution.[6]
>
> Smith paused and looked across the room at Singletary. He smiled slightly as he said:
>
> My honorable old daddy there won't think that I expect to be a Congressman and swallow up the liberties of the people. I never had any post nor do I want one. But I don't think worse of the Constitution because lawyers and men of learning and moneyed men are fond of it.[7]

Smith ended his remarks with words familiar to farmers:

> "There is a time to reap and a time to sow. We sowed our seed when we sent men to the Federal Convention. Now is the harvest."[8]

Still, the harvest didn't come easily in Massachusetts. Not until anti-Federalists Sam Adams and John Hancock endorsed a resolution calling for the immediate amendment of the constitution by adding a bill of rights, the so-called Massachusetts Compromise, did the convention manage a close vote of 187 to 168 in favor of ratification.

ARTICLE V

The ability to propose and adopt amendments to the constitution written in Philadelphia was a key factor in its ratification. Not only Massachusetts, but also New York and Virginia, ratified only on the assurance that a bill of rights would be immediately proposed as amendments.[9]

It is not a section of the Constitution that schoolchildren are required to memorize. Still, it is a vitally important Article of our national charter. Here is what Article V says:

> The Congress, whenever two-thirds of both Houses shall deem it necessary, shall propose Amendments to this Constitution, or on the Application of the Legislatures of two-thirds of the several States, shall call a Convention for proposing Amendments, which in either Case, shall be valid to all Intents and Purposes, as Part of this Constitution, when ratified by the Legislatures of three-fourths of the several States, or by Conventions in three-fourths thereof, as the one or the other Mode of Ratification may be proposed by the Congress; Provided that no Amendment which shall be made prior to the Year One thousand eight hundred and eight shall in any Manner affect the first and fourth Clauses in the Ninth Section of the first Article; and that no State, without its Consent, shall be deprived of its equal Suffrage in the Senate.[10]

As obscure as Article V may be to most Americans today, it was a pivotal point in the debates leading up to the ratification of the 1787 Constitution. In Connecticut, where the constitution was ratified by a comfortable 128 to 40 margin, delegate Richard Law called Article V:

> "an easy and peaceable way of amending any parts of the Constitution which may be found inconvenient in practice."[11]

In Massachusetts, ratification of the Constitution was not predicted. As the ratifying conventions gathered, newspapers carried the prediction that it would fail by a margin of about 48 votes. One of the proponents of ratification, Delegate James Bowdoin saw Article V as a rather quick fix to any problems:

> Like all other human productions, it may be imperfect: but most of the imperfections imputed to it are ideal and unfounded, and the rest are of such a nature that they cannot be certainly known but by the operations of the Constitution; and if, in its operation, it should in any respect be essentially bad, it will be amended in one of the modes prescribed by it. I say, will be amended, because the Constitution is constructed on such principles, that its bad effects, if any

> such should arise from it, will injure the members of Congress equally with their constituents; and, therefore, both of them must be equally induced to seek for, and effectuate, if possible, the requisite amendments.[12]

Bowdoin's sanguine estimate of the ease with which amendments would be approved has not exactly come to pass. Another supporter who was overly optimistic was Rufus King, who thought that:

> "gentlemen had not, in their objections to the Constitution, recollected that this article was a part of it: for many of the arguments of gentlemen were founded on the idea of future amendments being impractical."[13]

Like Bowdoin, he certainly could not have been thinking of a situation in which the members of Congress might be acting in total dereliction of the their Constitutional duties.

Doctor Charles Jarvis expressed "perfect approbation" and "complete satisfaction" with Article V and commented that it was the only example in history in which a revolution was accomplished "without public commotions" noting that most changes in the form of government had been "written in blood."

Much of the debate over ratification focused on the choice between adopting the Philadelphia draft or scrapping it and convening another convention to start all over again. Jarvis summed it up in these words:

> I shall not sit down, sir, without repeating, that, as it is clearly more difficult for twelve states to agree to another convention, than for nine to unite in favor of amendments, so it is certainly better to receive the present Constitution, in the hope of its being amended, than it would be to reject it altogether, with perhaps, the vain expectation of obtaining another more agreeable than the present.[14]

The weight and persuasiveness of such arguments are especially seen in the conversion of one Nathaniel Barrell. Along with sixteen other delegates from York County, Barrell was pledged to vote against ratification of the Constitution. On February 5, the day before voting began, Barrell addressed the Massachusetts convention and detailed a list of his objections to ratification. Then he closed with these words:

> But sir, although you may perceive, by what I have said, that this is not, in my view, the most perfect system I could wish, yet, as I am possessed with an assurance that the proposed amendments will take place; as I dread the fatal effects of anarchy, as I am convinced that the Confederation is essentially deficient, and that it will be more difficult to amend that than to reform this; and as I think this Constitution, with all its imperfections, is excellent, compared with that, and that it is the best constitution we can now obtain: I am

> almost tempted to risk [my constituents'] displeasure, and adopt it without their consent.[15]

The minutes of the convention show that Barrell did exactly that. He was the only delegate from York County to vote in favor of ratification.

CLASH OF TITANS

The ratification battle in Virginia is described by Biola University Professor Darren Patrick Guerra in his scholarly work *Perfecting the Constitution*, as the "clash of titans."

Patrick Henry, George Mason, James Monroe, and Richard Henry Lee opposed the constitution. Edmund Randolph, George Wythe, John Marshall, and James Madison argued in favor of ratification. Titans, indeed. Six of those men eventually had colleges named after them. But it was Patrick Henry who dominated the debate. Guerra quotes one historian as saying:

"Like a legendary swordsman of the people, single-handedly fending off an entire Royal Guard, Henry held the field for twenty-three days against future presidents, chief justices, cabinet officers, senators, diplomats. . . ."[16]

And further:

> Spectators and delegates alike sat frozen, hypnotized, as Henry ranged on and on, now thundering, now whispering, now threatening, now pleading. With masterful skill he found everyone's most vulnerable spot—his fears, principles, passions, prejudices—and pierced him there. . . . He portrayed the coming destruction of liberties so vividly that one spectator involuntarily felt his wrists to assure himself that the fetters were not already pressing his flesh. Even so worldly a pair of observers as Robert and Gouverneur Morris . . . sat awed by this man as if by one demonically inspired. Glumly, Madison wrote Hamilton that though the federalist had a majority of three or four delegates, he feared that Henry would carry the day.[17]

Henry argued from every direction. He questioned, for example whether Congress would ever cooperate in amendments that would be needed to control Congress, saying:

"However difficult it may appear, yet I must tell my opinion—that the most unworthy characters may get into power, and prevent the introduction of amendments."[18]

His conclusion: it would be too hard to amend the Constitution, an argument he bolstered by claiming that a "trifling minority" would be able to block amendments by refusing to ratify them.

When it was his time to take the floor, Madison made a rather obvious and persuasive point. Henry was complaining that the new Constitution would be too hard to amend, and yet he was arguing in favor of refusing ratification and leaving the Articles of Confederation in effect. Those Articles, Madison reminded the assembly, required unanimous agreement to be amended.

Henry was insisting that a bare majority ought to be able to amend the constitution. He pointed out that the Virginia Constitution permitted amendment by majority vote. That, in Henry's view, was the right way to do it. Madison, in effect, pointed out that Henry would make the best the enemy of the good, saying that amendment by nine states was at least better than requiring unanimous approval as was the case under the Articles of Confederation. Here is Madison:

> Have not experience and practice actually manifested this theoretical inconvenience to be extremely impolitic? Let mention one fact, which I conceive must carry conviction to the mind of any one: the smallest state in he Union has obstructed every attempt to reform the government; that little member has repeatedly disobeyed and counteracted the general authority; nay, has even supplied the enemies of its country with provisions. Twelve states had agreed to certain improvements which were proposed, being thought absolutely necessary to preserve the existence of the general government, but as these improvements, though really indispensible, could not, by the Confederation, be introduced into it without the consent of every state, the refractory dissent of that little state prevented their adoption. The inconveniences resulting from this requisition, of unanimous concurrence in alterations in the Confederation, must be known to every member in this Convention; it is therefore needless to remind them of them. Is it not self-evident that a trifling minority ought not to bind the majority? Would not foreign influence be exerted with facility over a small minority? Would the honorable gentleman agree to continue the most radical defects in the old system, because the petty state of Rhode Island would not agree to remove them?[19]

In due course, Virginia ratified the Constitution by a narrow margin, but not before news arrived that New Hampshire had become the critical ninth state to ratify the Constitution. The new nation was born, and the Commonwealth of Virginia simply had to be a part of it.

Hearing of Virginia's ratification, the opposition in New York folded. Even the intractable Melancton Smith threw in the towel and argued against a so-called conditional ratification which some were proposing as a guarantee that a bill of rights would be proposed and adopted. In the final analysis, Smith was confident that Article V would work.[20]

TRACK RECORD

There have been twenty-seven amendments added to the U.S. Constitution. All of them, and several which were never ratified, have been proposed by the Congress. Members of Congress introduce nearly 200 resolutions to propose constitutional amendments in every session. Over 11,000 proposed amendments have been introduced; only 33 were able to garner the necessary two-thirds vote in both Houses to be sent to the States for ratification. In the two hundred twenty-five years of our history, there has never been a convention as described in Article V.

Like many things that were done in the convention held in the summer of 1787 in Philadelphia, Article V was a compromise between those who wanted a strong national government and those who were afraid of a strong national government. The so-called Virginia Plan, which was, for practical purposes, the agenda for the Philadelphia Convention, specified that the constitution should have a provision allowing for its amendment. This was an important factor, since the Articles of Confederation had required unanimous consent to any amendment, a condition that was both impossible and paralyzing.

The Virginia Plan also specified that the national legislature ought to have no part in the amendment process. Alexander Hamilton disagreed and promptly drafted a resolution providing that amendments would be proposed by the Congress, then ratified by the states.

Virginia's George Mason objected strongly to the Hamilton draft. He argued that an oppressive Congress would never agree to propose amendments necessary to restrain a rogue, tyrannical legislature.

The draft of Article V was then changed to require that the Congress call a convention upon request of two-thirds of the state legislatures.

Mason still wasn't satisfied. By the time the convention reached its final days in mid-September, the Amendment provision had been added to Article V as it now reads. However, both methods were left in the hands (power) of the national legislature. Mason had objected to this back in June and now as the convention drew to a close, he rose to his feet to object. James Madison recorded:

> Col. Mason thought the plan of amending the Constitution exceptionable & amp; dangerous. As the proposing of amendments is in both the modes to depend, in the first immediately, in the second, ultimately, on Congress, no amendments of the proper kind would ever be obtained by the people, if the Government should become oppressive, as he verily believed would be the case.[21]

Mason was one of only three delegates to Philadelphia who refused to sign the Constitution on September 17, 1787. He later wrote that he saw the new government "eventually vibrating between a monarchy and a corrupt oppressive aristocracy."[22]

Although they went through the motions of amending Article V, the Federalists clearly won that debate. The States can ask for a convention, but

Congress must call it. An Article V convention can propose amendments, but Congress must decide how they are to be ratified.

So here is the unfortunate conundrum: Since Congress has the authority to propose constitutional amendments, the only reason for having an Article V convention is to propose amendments that the Congress will not propose.

It follows that the Article V convention is, by its very nature, an anti-Congress institution, inserted in the constitution for the very purpose of reining in a recalcitrant or overweening Congress. Most scholars and writers conclude that Article V is mandatory. After all, it says that when two thirds of the State Legislatures petition for a convention, the Congress SHALL call a convention.

But Congress is a parliamentary body. Representatives and Senators have the absolute right to vote as they choose, and if they choose not to do what the constitution requires them to do, there is no agency short of physical coercion that can force their hands.

Over the last 200 years, there have been more than 700 state applications for an Article V convention. Every State has asked; most several times. They have asked for different reasons; they have recited different causes and concerns; they have imposed various conditions and restrictions. But whatever their differences, the States have applied for the convention described in Article V, over and over and over again.

Bill Walker, a Washington state newspaper man, is the president of an organization called Friends of the Article V Convention. Its website, FOAVC.org is a cornucopia of information about Article V. It displays copies of 746 state petitions to Congress. The website also reports that counsel for the clerk of the House of Representatives, responding to a letter from FOAVC's Dan Marks, has opined that the clerk has not counted the applications for a convention because no statute has been passed requiring her to do so.

It would seem rather obvious that Congress is unlikely ever to heed State petitions for an Article V convention.

RUNNING AWAY

The constitution does not specify that applications for an Article V convention must be contemporaneous, or that they be addressed to the same purpose. The framers of the constitution were familiar with conventions, and they knew how conventions work. Indeed, they were sitting in a convention as they wrote Article V. They knew that conventions set their own agenda. They knew that the work of a convention involves compromise.

The founders understood that, even with Congress clinging to a tenuous veto, the primary rationale for creating a convention to propose amendments was to rein in the federal government. It was to give the states an avenue to iron out differences about how that goal can be achieved and a platform on which to approve the text of constitutional amendments.

That being the case, it makes no sense to insist that applications to Congress cannot be accumulated unless they agree on a specific amendment or an approved agenda.

Still, there are many voices heard throughout the land insisting that an Article V convention can and should be limited to considering a predetermined and defined agenda. Typically, these are not the voices of people who mean to obstruct or prevent a convention. On the contrary, they are folks who insist that they want the Congress to call an Article V convention, but only to do what they advocate and nothing else.

These are people who fear a "run away" convention. Unhappily, they reflect the majority opinion of the American people. A *Time* Magazine poll published in 2011 found that 65 percent of Americans believe that the constitution has "stood the test of time," while only 30 percent favored a new constitutional convention.[23]

Let's take a moment to reflect more carefully on the issue of a so-called "run away" convention. In the first place, a convention, by definition, is *sui juris*, a Latin phrase which basically means "a law unto itself." In law, *sui juris* is used to mean, "grown up," "fully responsible," "able to make his or her own decisions."

So when we say that a convention is sui juris, we mean that it is able to decide for itself what it will do. In short, a convention sets its own agenda. Period. That is what a convention does. That is what the word means. When the founders wrote "call a convention" they meant "call a constituent assembly that will set its own agenda."

Where, exactly do the proponents of a limited gathering derive their opinion? What was it about the 1787 convention or the constitution they wrote that would prompt anyone familiar with the English language to read into Article V the unspoken requirement that state petitions for a convention must be either contemporaneous or dedicated to the same agenda?

The writings of many scholars like Professor Rob Natelson, the Independence Institute's Senior Fellow in Constitutional Jurisprudence, typically begin by noting that the call for a convention is sent to the legislatures of the states. From that fact, they deduce that the convention is a meeting of delegates chosen by the state legislatures to represent the states.

Therefore, they reason, a convention being a constituent assembly, the constituents being represented by the delegates to the convention are the several states, speaking through their legislatures.

This is a fine point, but an important one. Are convention delegates assembled to represent the states or are they assembled to represent the people of the states? Here is how the delegates who framed the Articles of Confederation described themselves:

> To all to whom these Presents shall come, we the undersigned Delegates of the States affixed to our Names send greeting.
>
> Articles of Confederation and perpetual Union between the states of New Hampshire, Massachusetts-bay Rhode Island and Providence Plantations, Connecticut, New York, New Jersey, Pennsylvania, Delaware, Maryland, Virginia, North Carolina, South Carolina and Georgia.[24]

Clearly those delegates were convened to represent states, not people. That is what they said. That is what they did. They did not call the document they drafted a constitution. They knew what a constitution is. They knew that a constitution is the written expression of the consent of the governed—the people—so eloquently described in the Declaration of Independence as creating a new government, laying its foundation on such principles and organizing its powers in such form as to them shall seem most likely to effect their safety and happiness.

Admittedly, the delegates who gathered in Philadelphia were chosen by the state legislatures. But the fact that they were chosen by the legislatures does not mean that they were chosen to represent the legislatures. The legislators themselves were not elected to write a constitution for the United States. Had all the members of all the legislatures of all the states come together in one room, they would not have had the commission to write a constitution for a new nation.

Nations are created by the people. The people are sovereign. Legislatures are competent to select delegates to represent the people, but that does not mean that the delegates represent the legislatures or are beholden to the legislatures.

James Madison made the point quite vividly when writing to Edward Everett in 1830, saying of the 1787 Constitution:

> It was formed, not by the Governments of the component States, as the federal Government for which it was substituted was formed: nor was it formed by a majority of the people of the United States as a single community in the manner of a consolidated government.
>
> It was formed by the States—that is by the people in each of the States, acting in their highest sovereign capacity; and formed, consequently by the same authority which formed the State Constitutions.[25]

Chief Justice John Marshall, in the landmark case of *McCullough v. Maryland*, had this to say about the matter:

> Counsel for the State of Maryland have deemed it of some importance, in the construction of the Constitution, to consider that instrument not as emanating

> from the people, but as the act of sovereign and independent States. The powers of the General Government, it has been said, are delegated by the States, who alone are truly sovereign, and must be exercised in subordination to the States, who alone possess supreme dominion.
>
> It would be difficult to sustain this proposition. The convention which framed the Constitution was indeed elected by the State legislatures. But the instrument, when it came from their hands, was a mere proposal, without obligation or pretensions to it. It was reported to the then existing Congress of the United States with a request that it might "be submitted to a convention of delegates, chosen in each State by the people thereof, under the recommendation of the legislature, for their assent and ratification."
>
> This mode of proceeding was adopted, and by the convention, by Congress, and by the State legislatures, the instrument was submitted to the people. They acted on it in the only manner in which they can act safely, effectively and wisely, on such a subject—by assembling in convention. It is true, they assembled in their several States—and where else should they have assembled?
>
> No political dreamer was ever wild enough to think of breaking down the lines which separate the States, and of compounding the American people into one common mass. Of consequence, when they act, they act in their States. But the measures they adopt do not, on that account, cease to be the measures of the people themselves, or become the measures of the State governments.[26]

The preponderance of Americans who oppose a constitutional convention in spite of almost universal dissatisfaction with the way the national government functions, reflects the fact that Americans love the constitution more than they know it. One has only to visit the National Archives in Washington, DC to see the reverence with which the piece of paper on which the Constitution was written is preserved.

But ask the people who are lined up on Constitution Day to see the nation's charter on display to tell you what they know about the First Article of the Constitution and eight or nine out of ten will tell you that it protects freedom of speech or freedom of religion. They know about the First Amendment, but not about the First Article that establishes and empowers the Congress.

The American public is pitifully ignorant about the legal and historical facts that define the federal republic we call the United States of America. But you can't really blame them. Presidents, Senators, Congressmen, and Judges have all acquiesced in the transition of our nation from one of limited, defined powers to an omnipotent national sovereignty with the unchallenged authority to dictate every facet of human existence within our borders.

The problem, of course, is that the wolves have been in charge of the hen house.

FIXING THE GOVERNMENT

Most constitution buffs are familiar with the writings of Alexander Hamilton, James Madison, and John Jay under the pseudonym "Publius." They have been accumulated in what is known as The Federalist Papers.

Lesser known or cited are the letters of New York Chief Justice Robert Yates, who signed himself as "Brutus." An ardent anti-federalist, Yates expressed some fears that may have seemed exaggerated at the time, but which have proven quite prescient. Here is one. Citing the "Necessary and Proper" clause, Brutus opined:

> This government is to possess absolute and uncontrollable power, legislative, executive and judicial, with respect to every object to which it extends [effectively reducing] this country to one single government. And if they may do it, it is pretty certain they will; for it will be found that the power retained by the individual states, small as it is, will be a cog on the wheels of the government of the United States; the latter therefore will be naturally inclined to remove it out of the way. Besides, it is a truth confirmed by the unerring experience of ages, that every man, and every body of men, invested with power, are ever disposed to increase it, and to acquire a superiority over every thing that stands in their way. This disposition, which is implanted in human nature, will operate in the federal legislature to lessen and ultimately subvert the state authority.[27]

Does anyone question any more why the national government, headquartered in Washington, DC, just a few miles from the Atlantic Ocean, operates a Department of Housing and Urban Development, a Department of Health and Human Services, a Department of Agriculture, or a Department of Education and adopts laws, rules, and administrative regulations governing every facet of life in every city and village from Kennebunkport to San Diego?

Unhappily the march to nationalism has no organized opposition. The Democratic Party, while once claiming the states-centered mantles of Thomas Jefferson and Andrew Jackson, has long since adopted Franklin D. Roosevelt as its guiding star and national socialism as its long term goal.

Across the aisle, the Republican Party has never completely recovered from the Civil War. It is still the party of the Union, and is content to distinguish itself from the Democrats by a pro-business dedication to free enterprise as a national economic policy.

There is nobody in the nation's capital speaking for the domestic sovereignty of the American States. Members of the United States Senate, supposedly there to represent the several states, have become, mostly as a result of the Seventeenth Amendment, simply additional supplicants on behalf of the voters back home, Congressmen at large, if you will. Congressmen do not represent local communities. Their gerrymandered districts of manipulated constituencies define voters as racial, economic, and social blocs having nothing in common except the same Congressman.

Article V was intended to protect the domestic sovereignty of the American States. It is the last prerogative of the states to call the federal government to account and reassert their proper role in the governance of the people. Article V authorizes a convention, which, by definition, is a constituent assembly.

The Declaration of Independence asserts that government draws its legitimacy from the consent of the governed. A constitution is a compact among the people and between the people and their government that charters the government to use force for the common good.

The founders who met in Philadelphia began their constitution with these words: "We, The People of the United States." The history is clear. The Constitution of the United States of America was created by the people of the several states. An Article V convention contemplates a resort to first principles. It authorizes a convention of the people of the several states.

The people created the government. Only the people can fix the government.

SINGLE ISSUE EFFORTS

The vast majority of citizens and organizations who have advocated or are currently advocating an Article V convention support either a single amendment or a single subject, issue or topic to which the convention would be addressed and to which its deliberations would be limited.

Their reason for this approach is simple. They apprehend that a convention might, once convened, decide to consider one or more subjects not approved or contemplated by the state legislatures that applied for the convention.

State legislators are particularly wary of setting in motion a process over which they will have little or no control. Consequently, they too, insist on knowing, in advance, what the convention can and might do.

Quite typically, these convention proponents and the state legislators who agree with them would prefer that the Congress propose the amendment they seek. They solicit or endorse state applications in the hope that, as the count approaches the two-thirds goal, Congress will itself propose their amendment in order to avoid the necessity of calling convention.

Unhappily, that strategy is self-defeating. It assures that the various proponents will never really combine their efforts, despite honest attempts to cooperate. No one is advocating simultaneous conventions limited to different topics nor does anyone advocate combining topics, especially those that emanate from different points on the political compass.

Not only is the strategy self-defeating, it is also fraught with yet another sorry and unanticipated fault. One has only to recall the story of the 27th Amendment to understand the depths of the self-interest that has metastasized in the body politic. After two hundred years in limbo, the 27th Amendment, which prohibits members of Congress from raising their own salaries during their current term in office, was ratified in 1992. What did Congress do? On the very eve of the Amendment's ratification, they hastily gave themselves a COLA, an annual Cost of Living raise—which conveniently goes up but never down, every year.

Here is another example: Between May of 1957 and July of 1983, thirty-two state legislatures petitioned Congress for an Article V convention to propose a balanced budget constitutional amendment. Fearing that the critical number of thirty-four states—two-thirds of the fifty states—were about to demand a convention for the same purpose, the Congress promptly passed the Graham, Rudman, Hollings Act, an effort to impose automatic fiscal discipline on the federal government. The act was effective only to take the steam out of the push for a convention. The Act failed to balance the budget, promptly fizzled and was eventually repealed.

Over the next twenty years, however, thirteen states were convinced to rescind their petitions so that when Ohio petitioned in November of 2013, it was either the 33rd state or the 19th to favor a balanced budget convention, depending on whether the rescissions were deemed effective.

In March of 2014, the legislature of the State of Michigan adopted a resolution petitioning for an Article V convention to consider a balanced budget amendment. It was either the twentieth or the thirty-fourth state to do so, depending on the validity of the rescissions. This has touched off a debate about the validity of the rescissions. But Congress will not call a convention. Congress will assume that the rescissions are valid and leave the ball in the court of those who think otherwise. Proponents would then be forced to litigate the issue.

All of that takes time and money. When it finally reaches the United States Supreme Court, the issue will be decided by nine people who work for the national government and whose compensation is determined by the Congress. If they hold a wet finger to the wind, as they are often wont to do, they will assume that the rescissions, being more recent than the petitions rescinded, more nearly represent the current attitude of the state legislatures, and therefore a decision favoring the rescissions is more likely to be applauded as wise and judicious.

In the very unlikely possibility that the court might hold for the convention proponents and decide that 34 states are demanding a convention and that Congress is required to call the convention, what will Congress do? What else, but adopt a resolution that not only calls the convention, but also dictates its membership in a way that assures it will be friendly, if not subservient, to the Congress.

Examples are not difficult to conjure up. The resolution might say that the convention will consist of persons appointed by the Senators and Representatives from each state; one by each Senator and one by each Representative. Perhaps it would be more subtle, as saying that the delegations will be determined by state law, but sitting members of each state's Congressional delegation will attend the convention ex officio.

The point is indisputable to anyone familiar with the mindset of career politicians. It is simple, unvarnished common sense. The sciences of psychology, economics, sociology and law all teach us that self-interest is the principal motivator of human behavior. Members of Congress don't want to be required to balance the budget. They don't want to have their terms limited. They don't want any interference with the way they function. And they certainly don't want to call a convention which has the avowed purpose of reining in their prerogatives or dialing back their perquisites.

Patrick Henry, addressing the Virginia convention considering ratification of the constitution, insisted that Article V would never scale back an oppressive federal Congress. In his thundering oratorical fashion, Henry mesmerized the assembly with his words:

> Will the oppressor let go the oppressed? Was there ever an instance? Can the annals of mankind exhibit one single example where rulers, overcharged with power willingly let go the oppressed, though solicited and requested most earnestly? The application for amendments will therefore be fruitless. Sometimes, the oppressed have got loose by one of those bloody struggles that desolate a country, but a willing relinquishment of power is one of those things which human nature never was, nor ever will be, capable of.[28]

The Founders of our nation created the Article V convention option precisely as a means of amending the constitution in ways that Congress opposes. It is hardly surprising that Congress would refuse to cooperate in that effort.

WHY IT DOESN'T MATTER

Given that Congress will, under no circumstances, cooperate in the calling of a convention that might propose amendments deleterious to their privileges, powers and benefits, the question arises whether the call of Congress is in fact, necessary to the convening of an Article V convention for proposing amendments to the federal constitution.

The word "shall" occurs 267 times in the constitution and its amendments. The word "will" appears only three times. Typically, the word "shall" is used simply to indicate the consequence of an act or event or the effect of the adoption of the constitution itself. Thus, "... Powers granted herein shall be vested ..." "Taxes shall be apportioned ..." "each Senator shall have one vote ..."

It appears to have been used in the sense commonly intended in legal documents to express a future event or expectation as a synonym for "will." The word appears six times in Article V. Rather apparently, the first two times are more in the nature of conferring powers or predicting activities than mandating actions. Thus, whenever Congress "shall deem it necessary" Congress "shall propose amendments" sounds more like a recitation of expectations than a command or instruction.

Today, we might say something like, "when Congress thinks it is necessary, they will propose amendments." Seen in this light, the phrase "Congress ... shall call a Convention for proposing amendments" is not so much a mandate to the Congress as it is an expression of expectation that a convention will be called.

Putting it another way, the Founders were saying that if two thirds of the state legislatures want a convention, it will happen. In short, the phrase "Congress shall call a convention" means "Congress will call a convention," and is tantamount to saying "a convention will be called," Or "there will be a convention."

The true meaning of Article V is that two thirds of the states have the power to cause a convention to be held for the purpose of proposing amendments to the U. S. Constitution.

As much as that sounds very official and important, we have to ask the rather obvious questions, Who Can Propose an Amendment? Can't anybody do that? The word "propose" simple means to put forward, suggest, advance, offer or submit. Anybody can do that on a post card or on the Internet. Indeed, this book, like many others recently published, contains a number of proposals for amendment of the constitution.

Of course, some proposers are more effective and influential than others. Quite obviously, a constitutional amendment proposed by the legislatures of two thirds of the states would be more likely to be adopted than one proposed by a college fraternity.

It would seem to be equally apparent that amendments proposed by a convention consisting of delegates elected in each of the fifty states for the very purpose of proposing amendments, would also have considerable gravamen, whether the convention be recognized by Congress or not.

Whether authorized by the constitution or not, whether called by the Congress or not, whether recognized and approved by the state legislatures or not, amendments proposed by a convention would need to be ratified by three quarters of the states in order to become "for all intents and purposes" part of the federal constitution.

And it is the prerogative of the Congress to determine whether that ratification is by the legislatures in each of the states or by conventions in each of the states. So if a proposal comes from a convention that has not been called by the Congress, it would seem to have one of four fates.

First, it might simply go nowhere, and fade into the history books.

Second, it might be introduced in the Congress and either die there or be approved by two thirds of both houses and sent to the states for ratification.

Third, Congress might, by a simple majority vote in both houses, belatedly 'call' the convention, then, by the same simple majority, determine the mode of ratification as provided in Article V.

Fourth, the convention might send the proposal directly to the states, and ask that it be ratified by their legislatures and by conventions in each state as well. This process completely bypasses the Congress, and satisfies Article V by requiring ratification in both ways it specifies. This would obviously lead to a monumental constitutional crisis. While it might still be theoretically possible for the Congress to refuse to recognize the amendment, it is difficult to imagine that they would try to frustrate so overwhelming a national consensus.

Admittedly the untraveled road to constitutional reform via an Article V convention traverses uncharted terrain. Pockmarked with pitfalls and obstacles, it presents a daunting prospect for those who would answer the call for first responders.

And yet . . .

And yet it is an adventure of the heart for those who love the United States of America and revere her unique place in the history of human civilization. It may just be our last chance to save the Republic.

NOTES

1. Catherine Drinker Bowen, *Miracle at Phildelphia* (Little, Brown and Co, 1966) pp. 273–74.
2. U.S. Constitution, Article I, Section 8.
3. Bowen, *supra.*
4. Ibid.
5. Ibid.
6. Bowen, *supra,* p. 274.
7. Ibid.
8. Ibid.
9. Darren Patrick Guerra, *Perfecting The Constitution* (Lanham, MD: Lexington Books, 2013), p. 88.
10. U.S. Constitution, Article V.
11. Guerra, *supra,* p. 76.
12. Guerra, *supra,* p. 77.
13. Guerra, *supra.*
14. Guerra, *supra,* p. 78.
15. Guerra, *supra.* p. 79.
16. Guerra, *supra,* p. 80.

17. Guerra, *supra,* p. 82.
18. Ibid.
19. Guerra, *supra,* p. 85.
20. Guerra, *supra,* p. 91.
21. James Madison, *Notes of the Debates in the Federal Convention of 1787* (TeachingAmericaHistory.org).
22. Bowen, *supra,* p. 250
23. *Time*, July 4, 2011, Tenth Annual History Issue.
24. Preamble to the Articles of Confederation.
25. James Madison, "Letter to Edward Everett," August 28, 1830, in Ralph Ketcham, ed., *Selected Writings of James Madison* (Indianapolis, IN: Hackett, 2006) 340–48.
26. *McCullough v. Maryland,* 17 U.S. 316, 4 Wheat. 316, 4 L. Ed. 579 (1819).
27. Brutus, October 18, 1787, http://www.constitution.org/afp/brutus01.htm
28. Guerra, *supra,* p. 82.

Chapter Two

We Can and We Will

In 1785, a number of issues concerning navigation of the Potomac River and Chesapeake Bay prompted the States of Virginia and Maryland to have a meeting. Their delegates met with George Washington in his home at Mount Vernon.[1] They came away from that meeting persuaded that a larger gathering was necessary to address problems which all of the states were having under the Articles of Confederation.

Accordingly, the legislature of Virginia issued an invitation to the other twelve states to send representatives to the City of Annapolis on September 11, 1786 for what they called a *Meeting of Commissioners to Remedy Defects of the Federal Government.*

Four states ignored Virginia's call; Connecticut, Maryland, South Carolina, and Georgia. The other nine states appointed representatives, or commissioners, as they were called, but the commissioners representing only five states, actually showed up in Annapolis on September 11. The commissioners appointed by New Hampshire, Massachusetts, Rhode Island, and North Carolina, for whatever reason, did not arrive in Annapolis in time for the meeting.

There were twelve men at the Annapolis Convention. New York was represented by Alexander Hamilton and Egbert Benson; New Jersey by Abraham Clark, William C. Houston, and James Schureman; Pennsylvania by Tench Coxe; Delaware by George Read, John Dickinson, and Richard Bassett; and Virginia by Edmund Randolph, James Madison, Jr., and St. George Tucker.[2]

They met for three days, discussing the dire circumstances of the Confederation. They had come to Annapolis to talk about remedying the defects of the federal government. The only known minutes of the Annapolis meeting were taken by Egbert Benson of New York on September 11th.

Benson recorded that the convention appointed a committee consisting of Commissioners Benson, Clarke, Coxe, Read, and Randolph to draft a report on the work of the convention which could be delivered to the legislatures of the respective states that had sent them.

On comparing their credentials, the Annapolis Commissioners discovered that the New York, Pennsylvania and Virginia delegates had been given almost identical marching orders:

> to meet such commissioners as were, or might be, appointed by the other States in the Union, at such time and place, as should be agreed upon by the said Commissioners to take into consideration the trade and Commerce of the United States, to consider how far an uniform system in their commercial intercourse and regulations might be necessary to their common interest and permanent harmony, and to report to the several States, such an Act, relative to this great object, as when unanimously ratified by them would enable the United States in Congress assembled effectually to provide for the same. [3]

The delegates from New Jersey, however, carried slightly different instructions. Their charge was:

> To consider how far a uniform system in their commercial regulations *and other important matters* might be necessary to the common interest and permanent harmony of the several states. [4]

The committee reported the following day, September 12, and presumably there was discussion about their recommendations. Many historians believe that the original report of the committee was substantially modified at the insistence of Alexander Hamilton. It is well known that Hamilton had long been an advocate of a strong national government and had agitated for the calling of a convention to accomplish that purpose.

However it happened, or whoever led the charge, it is clear that the twelve commissioners who met in Annapolis, were not satisfied with discussing only commercial intercourse and regulations. Their final report cited the New Jersey resolution as "an improvement on the original plan."[5]

They knew they were stretching their marching orders, but they insisted that all of the states whose legislatures had sent them to Annapolis were certainly aware of "defects in the system" under the Articles of Confederacy. They said, in effect, that there was no need to make a list of the circumstances that required "an exertion of the united virtue and wisdom of all the members of the Confederacy," as the situation was both "delicate and critical."[6]

They concluded their report by urging the states that sent them to Annapolis to send delegates to Philadelphia on the second Monday in May of the following year, "to take into consideration the situation of the United States," and to "devise such further provisions as shall appear to them necessary to render the Constitution of the federal government adequate to the exigencies of the Union."[7]

They also asked their legislatures to do what they could to convince the other eight states to send delegates to Philadelphia as well. What happened next is critical to the efforts being advanced to convene an Article V Convention in the twenty-first century.

On November 23, 1786, the Commonwealth of Virginia authorized the appointment of delegates to the convention in Philadelphia.[8]

On November 24, 1786, the State of New Jersey authorized the appointment of delegates to the convention in Philadelphia.[9]

On December 30, 1786, the Commonwealth of Pennsylvania authorized the appointment of delegates to the convention in Philadelphia.[10]

On January 6, 1987, the State of North Carolina authorized the appointment of delegates to the Philadelphia convention.[11]

On February 3, 1787, the State of Delaware authorized the appointment of delegates to the Philadelphia convention.[12]

On February 10, 1787, the State of Georgia authorized the appointment of delegates to the Philadelphia convention.[13]

With those six states already committed to conducting a convention in Philadelphia in May, the Congress of the Confederation, on February 23, 1787, took up the matter and passed a resolution urging all of the States to send delegates to the Philadelphia convention.

Two days later, New York agreed to send a delegation. Massachusetts and South Carolina followed suit in March and, in May, Maryland and New Hampshire agreed as well. Only Rhode Island remained on the outside, and in fact, never sent a delegate to the Philadelphia convention.[14]

The simple truth these historical records demonstrate is that the convention at which the United States Constitution was drafted was *not called by the Congress*. It was called by the twelve men who met in Annapolis in September of 1786. What else is calling a convention other than setting the date, specifying the place, identifying the invitees, and sending out the invitations?

More needs to be said here on the question of what the delegates were sent to Philadelphia to do. It has been repeatedly represented that the Philadelphia convention was "illegal" in that, it is charged, the delegates were sent there merely to propose amendments to the Articles of Confederation, and not to write a constitution.

Nothing could be further from the truth. One has only to consult the resolutions of the state legislatures appointing delegates, to see what they were expected to do. Here, for example, is what the North Carolina legislature said:

> Whereas in the formation of the federal compact which frames the bond of union of the American states, it was not possible in the infant state of our republics to devise a system which in the course of time and experience would not manifest imperfections that it would be necessary to reform. And whereas the limited powers which by the articles of confederation are vested in the Congress of the United States, have been found far inadequate to the enlarged purposes which they were intended to produce. And whereas Congress hath by repeated and most urgent representations, endeavoured to awaken this and the other states of the union, to a sense of the truly critical and alarming situation into which they must be unavoidably cast, unless measures are forthwith taken to enlarge the powers of Congress, that they may thereby be enabled to avert the dangers which threaten our existence as a free and independent people. And whereas this state hath been ever desirous to act upon the enlarged system of the general good of the United States, without bounding its views to the narrow and selfish object of partial convenience, and has been at all times ready to make every concession to the safety and happiness of the whole, which justice and sound policy could vindicate:
>
> Be it therefore enacted by the General Assembly of the state of North-Carolina, and by the authority of the same, That five Commissioners be appointed by joint ballot of both Houses of Assembly, who, or any three of them, are hereby authorized as Deputies from this state, to meet at Philadelphia on the first day of May next, then and there to meet and confer with such Deputies as may be appointed by the other states for similar purposes, and with them to discuss and decide upon the most effectual means to remove the defects of our foederal union, and to procure the enlarged purposes which it was intended to effect, and that they report such an act to the General Assembly of this state, as when agreed to by them, will effectually provide for the same.[15]

The resolution of the Congress, and the resolutions of the various state legislatures concerning the Philadelphia convention authorized revising the system of governance, not merely amending the Article of Confederation.

THE CONNECTICUT COMPROMISE

The Annapolis commissioners set the place and the date, and determined that the thirteen states were to be invited to send delegates. The Congress of the Confederation did not set the date nor the place. Their invitation to the States was redundant, and while it may have added to the comfort level of the six States that had already agreed to send delegates, it was perfectly obvious to every member of the Congress of the Confederation that there was going to be a convention in Philadelphia on the second Monday in May, whether they passed a resolution calling for it or not.

What all the current advocates of an Article V convention must learn from this important historic precedent is that the States must first call the convention themselves, and then, like the Annapolis conferees did, invite the national Congress to give the convention its belated imprimatur.

The records of the convention of 1787 on September 10 show that James Madison remarked on the vagueness of the term "call a convention" in Article V. He wondered "How was a convention to be formed? By what rule decide? What the force of its acts?"[16]

Let us consider these three questions separately. The first question, "How is the convention to be formed?" can be answered by looking to the basic nature of the Article V convention. Its function is to propose amendments to the Constitution of the United States. Pretty obviously, therefore, the Article V convention must represent the same constituency as was represented in 1787. The Constitution was created by "We The People." It can only be amended by "We The People."

Who are the people who wrote the Constitution? The preamble describes them as "the People of the United States." The founders did not say "We The People of the United States of America." Why didn't they? They didn't because the United States of America had no people. The United States of America was the name of the confederation created by the Articles of Confederation. The Articles of Confederation were not a constitution. The Confederation they created was a "firm league of friendship" among the thirteen states. Like NATO or the UN, the league was nothing more than a treaty, an agreement among thirteen sovereign states. The United States of America in 1787 was not a nation. It did not have any citizens. It did not have any people.

So obviously, when the framers began the preamble with the words, "We the People of the United States" they meant to speak for the people of the thirteen original states. They did not speak for the thirteen state governments or for the thirteen state legislatures. They understood that a constitution is the solemn covenant by which the people give their consent to be governed. The principle of popular sovereignty was forcefully enunciated in the Declaration of Independence. Governments derive their just powers from the consent of the governed.

So Madison's first question is answered concisely that the convention is to be formed by the designation of delegates to represent the people of each of the States. The manner of designating delegates is left for the States to decide. They may hold conventions or elections or they may allow the governor or the legislature to appoint delegates. Whatever way may be chosen, the delegates do not represent the state governments or the state legislatures. They represent the people of the states.

Madison's second question "by what rule decide?" was anticipatory. A convention is *sui juris*. It makes its own rules. Nevertheless, there is a factor that goes to the heart of the amendment process that needs to be addressed at the very outset.

The convention of 1787 agreed upon what has been called 'the great compromise.' Sometimes referred to as the 'Connecticut compromise,' because it was suggested by Connecticut delegate Roger Sherman, the idea was to create a bi-cameral legislature in which one house would represent the people and the other house would represent the states, and to require the concurrence of both houses in order to pass any bill into law.[17]

The compromise was necessary because of the divergent interests of the larger and smaller states. The small states feared the larger states because, on a population basis, the larger states would have all the power, while the large states were equally fearful that a combination of small states would control decisions.

The dichotomy between small states and large states still exists. A majority of the American people reside in the ten most populous states. This fact necessarily impacts the entire process of amending the constitution, since it is theoretically possible for three quarters of the states, having less than half of the nation's people, to ratify a constitutional amendment. It is imperative therefore, that the convention be organized in such a way that the principle of the Connecticut Compromise will control the actions of the convention.

Here, however, we bump up against the fundamental fact that a convention is *sui juris* and makes its own rules. This raises the question of how the states can effectively design the convention so that it will favor adoption of a rule that echoes the Connecticut compromise.

The first prong of the convention compromise can be taken from the express words of Article V which requires the concurrence of three quarters of the states to adopt a constitutional amendment. It follows that any proposal for amendment should, at an absolute minimum, have the affirmative votes of three quarters of the states in the convention.

The second prong of the convention compromise would be the inclusion of a majoritarian requirement. This can be accomplished by the simple stratagem of inviting the several states not only to send a delegation to a named city on a specified date, but to couch that invitation in terms which establish the size of the state's delegation. In this fashion, an organizational committee on credentials will determine whether a state is represented by the appropriate number of delegates before they are seated.

THE 50K PLAN

Now the question arises, how to decide the number of delegates to be sent by each state. Here we have some guidance from the nation's founders.

Along with the Bill of Rights, two other constitutional amendments were proposed by the Congress in 1788. One of them, prohibiting members of Congress from giving themselves annual pay increases sat in limbo for two hundred years until it was ratified as the 27th Amendment.

The other 1788 proposal that was not ratified with the Bill of Rights was called Article the First. It specified a formula for determining the size of the House of Representatives in relation to the population of the United States. Unfortunately, there was a scrivener's error in the proposal as published. It provided that the House should have a minimum of 200 members and a maximum of one member for every fifty thousand inhabitants.

When the population reached eight million, that proposal became mathematically and rationally impossible, since the maximum would then be 160, forty members LESS than the minimum of 200.

As a result, Article the First was never ratified, and the size of the House of Representatives was left to be established from time to time by ordinary legislation. We will discuss the impact of that situation later. For the present, though, it is important to note that James Madison and the members of the first Congress were of the opinion that a ratio of one representative for every 50,000 constituents was a reasonable standard of representative government.

In 1787 when the Founders agreed on a ratio of approximately one representative for every 30,000 inhabitants, the English House of Commons had 275 members representing a population of about eight million, a ratio of just under 29,000 to one. No doubt that ratio was a model noted by the Founders. Today, the House of Commons consists of 650 people for a population of just over 63 million, a ratio of one MP to slightly under one hundred thousand people.

While Article the First was never ratified, it was nonetheless expected by everyone that the size of the House of Representatives would grow as the population grew. In point of fact, Section 2 of Article I of the Constitution provides:

> "Representatives and direct Taxes shall be apportioned among the several States which may be included within this Union, according to their respective Numbers . . ." [18]

In 1787, each State determined for itself how many delegates to send to the Philadelphia convention. The relative size of the state delegations didn't matter because voting was by states, and not by representatives. Each state had one vote in the convention, just as they did in the Confederation Congress. The representatives from each state decided among themselves how their state's vote would be cast.

An interesting sidelight: the Philadelphia convention was attended by 55 delegates. The population of the United States at that time was approximately 2,750,000. Thus the ratio of population to delegates at the Philadelphia Constitutional Convention was very close to 50,000 to one.

The 1787 convention worked against the backdrop of state by state voting in the Confederation Congress. It was the system they were accustomed to, and it was the default system which would remain in effect unless changed.

In 2014, the backdrop is different. The system of voting in Congress, being the result of the Connecticut Compromise, requires concurrence of both a popular vote and a state by state vote. That is the default system, which will remain in place unless and until it is changed.

The convention compromise then, should recognize this status quo, and incorporate both means of voting by a rule that no amendment be approved by the convention unless it receives the affirmative votes of the delegations of three quarters of the states and, concurrently, of a majority of all the delegates to the convention.

Using the standard proposed by James Madison and adopted by the House of Representatives in 1788, the convention would have one representative for every 50,000 inhabitants. Against the national population according to the 2010 census, that would mean a total of 6,163 delegates. When calculated state by state, the total is 6,166.

The idea of a deliberative body consisting of 6,166 people usually strikes listeners as a cumbersome, unworkable, noisy crowd like a partisan nominating convention of the annual gathering of the Friendly Sons of Saint Patrick.

But that picture is wrong. In the first place, modern technology enables a large body to function remotely. Only a very small percentage of the delegates need actually assemble. What they say and do would be broadcast to delegates participating in their home states using their computers. That system would hardly be a change from the present practice of Members making speeches before a roomful of empty chairs.

George Mason, a Virginia delegate to the convention of 1787, made this comment about republican government:

> To make representation real and actual, the number of representatives ought to be adequate; they ought to mix with the people, think as they think, feel as they feel—ought to be perfectly amenable to them, and thoroughly acquainted with their interest and condition.[19]

Fifty thousand people is about the outer limit of most people's range of familiarity. If you are from Midland or Battle Creek, and you meet some folks from your hometown while visiting Disney World, chances are fair that if you don't know them you know someone who does.

So a delegate selected from a community-based district of 50,000 people is likely to be well-acquainted with the interest and condition of the constituents. More importantly, a sample of six thousand one hundred sixty-six delegates, evenly distributed across the nation, will produce a statistically reliable reading of the sentiments of the nation.

In the matter of amending the national constitution, this reading is critical. Constitutions must be written in the plain language of the people. They must be read and understood by the broad mass of the citizenry. Written constitutions must say what they mean and mean what they say.

Delegates are not selected at random from the community, like jurors. They are elected or appointed on the assumption and with the expectation that they will engage in the deliberative process, which involves reading, listening and asking questions. They are decision makers, oath bound to devote their best efforts to the parliamentary process. Their votes should reflect the choices that their constituents would make, given the same exposure to information and debate.

Given that Congress will never agree to call a convention, and given that logically, legally, and informed by historical precedent, an Article V Convention can, and, indeed ought to be called by the states themselves, the conclusion is that one or more state legislatures should initiate the call by adopting a resolution setting the date and place for the convention to occur and urging the other states to do likewise, at the same time incorporating in the call the essentials of the convention compromise.

The resolution would look something like this:

Resolution in Support of a Convention
To Propose Amendments
To The United States Constitution

WHEREAS, The Constitution of the United States provides in Article V for the calling of a convention for the purpose of proposing amendments as an alternative to proposals offered by the Congress; and,

WHEREAS, There are a number of serious concerns with respect to the operation of the national government and its relationship with the several States which the People of the States wish to address in the manner envisioned by the Founders of the nation;

NOW THEREFORE, The House of Representatives of the State of _______________, the Senate concurring, does hereby RESOLVE:

That this State shall participate, in the manner hereinafter prescribed, in a convention to be conducted in the City of Saint Louis in the State of Missouri beginning on the second Monday in May, ______, for the purpose of proposing, by vote of the majority of all delegates thereto, a super-majority of three quarters of the state delegations concurring, such amendments to the Constitution of the United States as shall be deemed proper and useful.

1) That _____ delegates shall be selected in such manner as shall be provided by law, to represent the people of this state at such convention, being one delegate for every 50,000 inhabitants as found by the decennial census of 2010.

2) That a copy of this resolution be conveyed to the Speaker of the House of Representatives of each of the several States of the United States, with the request that a similar resolution be offered and considered therein,

3) That a copy of this resolution be conveyed to the Congress of the United States with the request that it shall call the convention described herein in accordance with Article V of the United States Constitution.

FIRST RESPONDERS

Members of state legislatures are not prone to crawl out on political limbs. The idea of calling or participating in an Article V convention which has not been officially called by the United States Congress is not likely to sweep to instant majorities on the floors of the fifty state legislatures. The usual die-hard opponents of constitutional reform will scream about "run away" conventions and posit all manner of horror stories to stifle the effort.

Still, there is a humor in the land. The people want something to be done, and that something has to be done in the foundational charter of our liberties, the Constitution of the United States of America.

It is time for the First Responders to respond. It is time for volunteers to rush to the ramparts. Like chain gangs passing sand bags hand to hand to shore up the river dykes, the people of the United States must undertake the tedious, messy, unheralded, wearisome work of generating support for the convention.

Some of them have already stepped up. You can find them on the Internet at any number of sites, spreading one version or another of the common song of liberty under law. Not a few of them have joined Convention USA.

The international distress call of "mayday" is derived from the French expression, "venez m'aider" meaning "Come to My Aid." It is used mostly by seamen and aviators to call for help in life threatening situations. In the United States, we are keenly familiar with the significance of "nine one one"—the telephone number that summons First Responders to all sorts of emergencies.

There is a universal force that compels response to a call for help. It taps the fundamental social dimension of the human survival instinct. A distress signal has the same physical effect as directly perceived personal danger. Adrenalin flow jumps. The heart races. The senses become more acute. Run, don't walk. Step up. Stand up.

We have all been First Responders at one time or another. Some of us are quick and eager to help. Some of us, perhaps most of us, really don't want to get involved. We would honestly rather not hear the call, which is why sailors yell "mayday, mayday, mayday." They always say it three times, so there is no mistake. And it's why the 911 operator has to make sure the call is real and the need is urgent.

To be a First Responder, you have to hear the call for help. Sometimes that takes serious listening. The founders of our nation intended every subsequent generation to be "We the People." They expected that down through the years, patriotic citizens would step up and do what needs doing so that government "of the people, by the people and for the people" would not perish from the earth.

But that call does not bang against our eardrums. It addresses our hearts and our minds. It sends a quiet, constant, drip, drip, drip kind of distress signal, like the tapping of a coal miner trapped hundreds of feet below the surface of the earth, hoping against hope that someone will hear. That someone will come.

Many Americans have heard the tapping. They know that something is wrong. Liberals, conservatives, progressives, and libertarians; Republicans, Democrats, and Independents, are all complaining about the national government; discontent is endemic. The time has come to stand up and be counted.

Nearly 400 First Responders have registered at www.conventionusa.org, They are willing to serve on a citizens' jury of 6,166 delegates from all around the nation. They are ready to study, discuss, debate, and decide upon proposed amendments to the U.S. Constitution.

Delegates to Convention USA are not anonymous. They register their name, home address, date of birth, phone number, and email address. They certify that they are registered voters. They take an oath to support the constitution. They stand up to be counted, and their votes are recorded.

Who are these people? What kind of people would go on the Internet and make such a commitment to be identified with an extraordinary constitutional convention that has not been called by Congress? What kind of people want their state legislatures to send delegates to a convention that has not been called by Congress? Who are they? Here are a few of them:

David Biddulph is a seventy-year-old former Detroit banker who moved with Susie, his wife of forty-eight years, to Florida where they launched a solar heating company. In the late 1980s his mother-in-law was forced to move from her Florida retirement home because the real estate taxes went from $800 to $4,800 in a matter of six years. Concerned about this draconian rise in tax assessments, Biddulph volunteered to lead the "Save Our Home" petition drive in Volusia County.[20]

His efforts paid off. On Super Tuesday in 1992 he organized sixty volunteers who gathered 15,000 signatures in one day. He went on to coordinate the state-wide petition drive that resulted in a 3 percent assessment limitation measure being placed on the 1992 Florida ballot. It passed with a 54 percent majority and now saves taxpayers over $6 billion a year.

David Biddulph is a First Responder, not an officeholder, or an office seeker. Not a pleader for special interests or special privilege, he saw a need for citizen action and he acted. His reward was the knowledge that his effort made a difference.

That same motivation has prompted him to register as a delegate to Convention USA. Biddulph is just one of nearly 400 Americans who have stepped forward to participate in Convention USA.

Merlin Fields is a radio show host, a progressive Democrat in Tennessee. He has written in support of a convention in such liberal publications as Daily Kos. Victor Flores is a registered Republican in Texas, a recent law school graduate, and a Hispanic Latino helping to mobilize the Republicans in McAllen.

David Keller is a Vermont farmer and small business owner. Lamont Andrews is a dedicated Christian conservative in Arizona, and Joshua Arrowood of Tennessee is a dad, a husband, a school teacher, a coach, a libertarian, and a constitutionalist.

Thomas Ash of Maryland wants a balanced budget. Laurie Atkinson has lived in the same Michigan house for fifty years. She loves the outdoors, her state, and her country, and she thinks the time has come to return power to the people.

Virginia Bahs is an Air Force veteran from Ohio with two grown children, Curtis Bard of New York just wants to help, and David Arver is a Michigan broadcaster who hopes to see the country returned to its roots as a republic instead of being hitched to a yoke in support of corporate interests.

Tom Boese is a truck driver and Clayton Biewer is an accountant. They're both from Wisconsin. Annette Boyd is an elected official in Illinois and Matthew Blackman is an attorney in New Jersey.

George Bevill of Knoxville is concerned about the way our government does business, and Rebecca Brigandi from Nevada wants her children and grandchildren to live free in a constitutional republic.

And there are more.

COMMON SENSE; COMMON PEOPLE

Stoney Ferguson is a Michigan man. He has this to say:

> I was a Democrat but have decided after some serious reflection I really have always been an independent. I believe politics should be taken more seriously than which team, i.e: Dems or Repubs, is going to be the most popular at the polls. I believe this country should be united instead of divided. "Integrity" is doing the right thing even when no one is looking. This should be the standard that "We the People" need to look for in every elected official who represents us.

Lawrence Dunbar, a veteran who served in the armed forces under five presidents, is a concerned parent and grandparent who believes that we must rein in the government and take our country back.

Sally Elkardy is a New York City councilwoman who is deeply concerned about the threat to the constitutional rights of all Americans that is posed by the National Defense Authorization Act.

Robert Frank of Stockbridge, Michigan is worried about the influence of the United Nations on our domestic laws, and Michael Gunn is a USAF veteran with twenty years in law enforcement who believes the Constitution is set in stone.

Joseph Groppe is the director of music at a Florida Catholic church who thinks that the periodic debt ceiling circus shows how dysfunctional the government is, and Lewis Harper is a Florida lawyer who quotes James Madison saying that there are more instances of the abridgement of the freedom of the people by gradual and silent encroachments of those in power than by violent and sudden usurpations.

Dennis Harbert is a sixty-seven-year-old retired businessman from Massilon, Ohio who awoke from political slumber in 2008 and has concluded that a constitutional convention is the only way to save the Republic from the enemies within.

Sherry McKenzie has her PhD in education. She is the principal of a K–12 school in a small village in Alaska. She believes in helping others to take responsibility for their choices. Brett McGraw is from Durham, North Carolina. He calls himself a Constitutionalist and a classical liberal Goldwater Conservative. He believes in Liberty, Reason, and Knowledge.

Thomas Hart of Conroe, Texas is a veteran and a retired firefighter. A student of the Constitution and history, he has been fighting for conservative causes since age fifteen. James Headrick of Jonesborough, Tennessee, who wrote a book titled *Repair and Upkeep of the United States Constitution*, doesn't think either political party abides by the Constitution.

Andy Hawks of Sussex, Delaware has been practicing Law for twenty-eight years. He has made constitutional law an avocation for twenty years and currently writes a blog about the process of constitutional amendment.

An active participant in Occupy Owensboro, Tennessee, Ryan Hidalgo is a twenty-eight-year-old activist who very much wants to be part of the process of assuring major changes in our country, and Thomas Jackson is a First Responder who has fought shipboard fires in the boiler room. He would stand and fight, if necessary.

Thomas Jedrzejewicz of Los Angeles, California writes:

> I believe that government needs to be guided by two premises: individual liberty and effectiveness. I think America has too much heart to be really libertarian. I think we need to evaluate whether social programs are working,

> and I think we need to recognize that taxes are collected at gun point and consider that fact when choosing to spend.

A mineralogist from Edison, New Jersey, Lois Johnson would rather look at crystals than the antics of people, but as an American, she fully supports the Constitution and does not want to see it undermined by political antics.

Delegate Michael Ferris of Arizona writes:

> I am an American citizen trying to run a small business in a country that has been poorly managed and is broke. The only way the government can see to fix this problem is to take more of the revenue from the producers by way of regulatory agencies. I have educated and continue to educate myself in the forging of our great nation and in the principles of our Founding Fathers and it is obvious that history is repeating itself. I believe it is once again time to return The United States of America to the People. An Article V Convention seems like the only option with the immediate results necessary to regain control of the federal government and I am dedicated to do whatever I can to help its cause.

Kenneth Fendler, a delegate from California, expressed agreement with these words of Thomas Jefferson:

> I consider the foundation of the Constitution as laid on this ground that "all powers not delegated to the United States by the Constitution, nor prohibited by it to the States, are reserved to the States, or to the people. To take a single step beyond the boundaries thus specially drawn around the powers of Congress, is to take possession of a boundless field of power, no longer susceptible of any definition."[21]

An Article V Convention must summon the common sense of common people. The Constitution of 1787 was written in the plain language of the people. Indeed, it begins with the words, "We the People." it was published verbatim in newspapers throughout the country. The people read it. The people debated it. The people understood it. And the people ratified it in conventions held in every state.

The goal should be to choose 6,166 delegates from districts designated all over America. The object is to assemble a critical mass of common sense. People who are competent to make life and death decisions as members of a jury are equally able to read and understand the words of the constitution and its amendments.

THE UNWASHED

The lives of most Americans revolve around mundane daily pursuits; eat and sleep, work and play, laugh and cry, live and die. Sunday morning church.

Monday night football. Family and friends. Labors and neighbors. They do their own thing, mind their own business, have their own opinions.

Average Americans are the targets of incessant communication. People tend to be swayed by repetition, which is why telephone numbers are repeated five or six times in so many commercials. In national and state-wide elections most voters are influenced by television, newspapers, or mass communication by mail or on the Internet.

Local elections are different. Voters often know the candidates personally or through mutual connections. Personal contact is important. Party affiliation is still important, but not as crucial as it is in larger elections.

Curiously, there is one factor that the campaign managers can't influence very much, and that is what a person looks like. That's right. People tend to vote for candidates just because they "like his or her looks."

Princeton psychologist Alexander Todorov demonstrated this phenomenon back in 2006, when he showed that quick judgments, based on looking at pictures of candidates' faces can accurately predict real-world election returns.

Todorov's lab tests involved showing pictures of candidates to a number of people unfamiliar with the elections. Their rapid appraisal of competing candidates' faces was sufficient to predict the winner in about 70 percent of races for U.S. senator and state governor in the 2006 elections.[22]

Instinct? Experience? Training? Maybe all those and more. I was a trial Judge. In my experience, the jury was usually right. One of the instructions we gave to jurors was that they are the sole judges of the truthfulness of the witnesses and that they were expected to use their own experiences in life, their own visceral reactions, to help them decide who was telling the truth.

People are the best experts on people. In the same way, there is such a thing as common sense. I like to call it "the intuitive wisdom of the great unwashed." More appropriately, it is the common sense of the common folks.

Public opinion isn't stupid, but it can be and often is misrepresented, and, unhappily, the misrepresentation itself becomes the catalyst for manipulating public opinion.

If you ask 1,000 people if they think a woman should be put in jail for having an abortion, 999 will probably say "No." But that result does not support a news story under the headline "99.9 Percent Favor Abortions."

Anti-abortion laws always punished the people who performed abortions, not the women who had them. If you ask people if they think medical doctors should lose their licenses for performing abortions, the answers would most likely be "no" by a slight margin, but if the question is whether dentists or podiatrists or midwives should be forbidden to perform abortions, the poll would surely tip toward a majority of "yes" answers.

My point is that public opinion is volatile and always reacts to the manner in which the issue is framed. Words matter. A constitution must mean what it says and say what it means. If it does, and if it expresses what the people intend and want, it will be widely accepted.

Constitutional amendments need the almost universal consensus of the American people in order to be adopted. What is important is whether the amendment at issue is framed accurately and in the plain words most people understand.

Even more important is whether the amendment was written by someone they know and trust. A convention which is comprised of delegates elected or appointed from their local city, town, or county will have credibility.

Some people who oppose the convention like to say that there are no more George Washingtons, James Madisons, or Alexander Hamiltons in America.

Here's what Alexander Hamilton had to say about that:

> I never expect to see a perfect work from imperfect man. The result of the deliberations of all collective bodies must necessarily be a compound, as well of the errors and prejudices as of the wisdom and good sense of the individuals of whom they are composed.[23]

Thomas Jefferson had a similar opinion. In a letter to Samuel Kercheval dated July 11, 1816, he wrote:

> Some men look at constitutions with sanctimonious reverence, and deem them like the Ark of the Covenant, too sacred to be touched. They ascribe to men of the preceding age a wisdom more than human, and suppose what they did to be beyond amendment. I knew that age well; I belonged to it, and labored with it. It deserved well of its country. It was very like the present, but without the experience of the present; and forty years of experience in government is worth a century of book reading; and this they would say themselves were they to arise from the dead.[24]

Convention delegates should come from every point on the political compass. Many, of course, will have special expertise. There were many lawyers in Philadelphia two hundred and thirty years ago. Certainly, lawyers, scholars, teachers, and public officials, both current and retired, will be interested. Many who have written books about Article V should be heard.

The First Responders, who have registered at Convention USA, include activists in the Republican Party, the Democratic Party, the Tea Party, and the Occupy Movement. They describe themselves as constitutionalists, conservatives, progressives, liberals, and libertarians. The one thing that unites them is the common belief that a convention can do good work, that it can make a difference, that it will be a platform from which the people of the states can speak and be heard.

We have joined hands with strangers, whose commitment to our nation makes them our brothers and sisters. I could not express our mission better than Warren Tape of Santa Rosa, Florida. Forty-eight years old, married 21 years, and a father of three sons, Warren wrote this when he registered as a delegate:

> About three years ago, I began to seriously read on the subject of history. The piece that first captured my interest was Thomas Paine's "Common Sense," and wanting a greater understanding, followed it up with "Declaration: The Nine Tumultuous Weeks When America Became Independent, May 1-July 4, 1776" by William Hogeland and "Ratification: The People Debate the Constitution, 1787–1788" by Pauline Maier. As I continued to read on early American history, three things quickly impressed me: First, that the success of our nation is rooted in the founding fathers' understanding of history, second, that there is very little in the difficulties our nation faces that the founding fathers' did not anticipate and third, that what we were taught in school in American history missed everything that is most important for Americans to know.
>
> Thomas Jefferson wrote, "What country can preserve its liberties if its rulers are not warned from time to time that their people preserve the spirit of resistance?"[25] To expect government to restrain itself according to the law is to repudiate history.
>
> The great difficulty in the People's ability to check the power of government, the instrument of our paralysis, is an appearance that we are so intractably divided by our separate interests that finding the basic agreement needed to address the problem is impossible. George Washington described the problem in his Farewell Address when he wrote, "One of the expedients of party to acquire influence, within particular districts, is to misrepresent the opinions and aims of other districts. You cannot shield yourselves too much against the jealousies and heart-burnings, which spring from these misrepresentations; they tend to render alien to each other those, who ought to be bound together by fraternal affection."
>
> While Amendments to the Constitution may not be in order, if the People can require Congress to call a Convention to propose Amendments, the Convention's greatest good will be as a means for us to demonstrate to ourselves that we are capable of uniting in common cause and that when we do, government must bow to our will.

SAINT LOUIS

In 1904, the City of Saint Louis celebrated the centennial of the Louisiana Purchase by hosting a World's Fair. Spread over more than 1,200 acres and comprised of 1,500 buildings connected by nearly 75 miles of roads and walkways, the fair attracted almost 20 million visitors between April and December.[26]

Forty years later, Metro Goldwyn Mayer resurrected the Fair in a motion picture entitled "Meet Me in Saint Louis" starring Judy Garland. Over the years, that title has become a kind of idiom suggesting compromise—meeting someone half way, finding a common or neutral place or decision.

The geographical center of the population of the United States is about 3 miles from Plato, Missouri. It's a town of 109 souls roughly 150 miles southwest of Saint Louis. Plato doesn't have a convention center, but Saint Louis does.

An Article V amendatory constitutional convention will have to bring together Americans of every political opinion, left, right, radical, mainstream, conservative, liberal, traditional, and innovative. To accomplish anything, they will have to find common ground. They will have to meet figuratively, at least, in Saint Louis.

Americans are pragmatic. Whenever an Article V amendatory constitutional convention is mentioned, their first reaction is to ask what amendment or amendments it would propose. It would be well if supporters of the convention would take a page from the Annapolis convention. Here is what they said:

> Your commissioners decline an enumeration of those national circumstances on which their opinion respecting the propriety of a future convention, with more enlarged powers, is founded; as it would be a useless intrusion of facts and observations, most of which have been frequently the subject of public discussion, and none of which can have escaped the penetration of those to whom they would in this instance be addressed. They are, however, of a nature so serious as, in the view of your commissioners, to render the situation of the United States delicate and critical.[27]

The disposition of the American people to call our elected officials to account for their conduct of the nation's business has never been more acute. The litany of our common grievances against the ruling elite of the twenty-first century rivals the recitation of the causes of rebellion that were detailed in the Declaration of Independence:

They have gerrymandered elective districts to deny citizens of local communities the right to be represented:

They have neglected and refused for more than one hundred years to obey the mandate of Article I, Section 2 of the Constitution which requires that members of the House of Representatives be apportioned among the several states according to their respective numbers:

They have failed and refused to adopt budgets year after year:

They have repeatedly appropriated more money than held in the treasury:

They have authorized borrowing incomprehensible amounts of money with neither the ways nor the means to repay:
They have suffered the credit of the United States to be downgraded in the marketplace:
They have abdicated their responsibility to decide when the nation shall go to war, against whom, and for what purpose:
They have permitted the Executive to make laws, suspend laws, and ignore laws:
They have adopted legislation without reading it or knowing what it contained:
They have repeatedly adopted omnibus legislation filled with special appropriations, tax breaks and incentives favoring particular interests:
They have used the power and prerogatives of their offices to placate corporate interests:
They have consorted with lobbyists and granted special favors of every stripe:
They have voted annual raises for themselves, for the avowed purpose of circumventing the Twenty-Seventh Amendment:
They have suffered the government of the United States to be shut down, denying needed services and opportunities to the people:
They have created a nominal debt ceiling and repeatedly raised it:
They have repeatedly failed and refused to act collegially, making no effort to compromise for the common good, but have instead indulged in partisan invective and opprobrium:
They have demeaned the federal judiciary by injecting banal partisanship into the process of nominating and confirming judges:
They have appointed and confirmed judges who have presumed to make laws ex cathedra without any controversy pending before them
They have permitted federal judges to invade the domestic sovereignty of the several states and to exercise powers reserved to the states:
They have abdicated the office of legislators by permitting members of the executive department to promulgate copious, tutelary administrative regulations with which to harass our people:
They have encroached upon the domestic sovereignty of the several states by adopting laws concerning matters properly and historically reserved to the jurisdiction of the states:
They have, after more than two centuries of honored tradition, abolished the accepted parliamentary rule requiring a super majority vote to terminate debate, thus silencing minority voices in the United States Senate:

In sum, the Congress of the United States has so conducted its affairs as to earn the disapproval of ninety percent of the American people, exacerbating the frustration and alienation of the citizens from their government.

It is time for a convention. Verily, the time has come. The Founders of our nation knew it would come. Thomas Jefferson said it:

> if once the people become inattentive to the public affairs, you and I and Congress and Assemblies, Judges and Governors, shall all become wolves. It seems to be the law of our general nature, in spite of individual exceptions.[28]
> He also observed:
> No other depositories of power but the people themselves have ever yet been found, which did not end in converting to their own profit the earnings of those committed to their charge.[29]

George Washington is often reputed to have said:

> "government is not reason; it is not eloquence. It is force. And force, like fire, is a dangerous servant and a fearful master."[30]

Not everyone in the room on September 17, 1787 signed the constitution. George Mason of Virginia didn't. He saw the government it created as vibrating between a monarchy and a corrupt, oppressive aristocracy. Maybe Ben Franklin did too. Our nation, he said, is a republic, "if you can keep it."[31]

The founders realized that power corrupts; that money and power attract and poison each other; that men seek power to get money and use money to get power. That is why they gave us a way to push back when the federal government gets out of hand. It's right there in Article V of the United States Constitution.

NOTES

1. Known as the Mount Vernon Compact, it was the first effort to improve the Articles of Confederation.
2. Proceedings of Commissioners to Remedy Defects of the Federal Government; *The Avalon Project,* Lillian Goldman Law Library, Yale University Law School.
3. William Benton, ed. *The Annals of America,* Vol. 3, 1784–1796 (Encyclopedia Britannica, 1968), p. 69.
4. Ibid.
5. Benton, *supra,* p. 20
6. Ibid.
7. Ibid.
8. *The Documentary History of the Ratification of the Constitution, Digital Edition*, eds. John P. Kaminski, Gaspare J. Saladino, Richard Leffler, Charles H. Schoenleber, and Margaret A. Hogan (Charlottesville: University of Virginia Press, 2009).
9. Ibid.
10. Ibid.
11. Ibid.
12. Ibid.

13. Ibid.
14. Ibid.
15. *The Documentary History of the Ratification of the Constitution,* Canonic URL: http://rotunda.upress.virginia.edu/founders/RNCN-01-01-02-0006-0005-0001 [accessed 11 May 2011]
16. Guerra, *supra,* p. 72.
17. U.S. Constitution, Article I, Section 7.
18. U.S. Constitution, Article I, Section 2.
19. Brion McClanahan, *The Founding Fathers Guide to the Constitution* (Washington, DC: Regnery, 2001), p. 210.
20. The stories of Mr. Biddulph and others recounted here are taken from profiles inserted by the delegates at the website www.conventionusa.org. They are available for viewing by fellow delegates, but not by the general public. The author has included them here with the approval or acquiescence of the delegates.
21. Thomas Jefferson, "Letter to George Washington on the Constitutionality of the Bank of the United States," 1791.
22. *Science* vol. 308, no. 5728, pp. 1623-26. 10 June 2005: DOI: 10.1126/science.1110589.
23. Alexander Hamilton, Federalist #85.
24. Thomas Jefferson, "Letter to Samuel Kercheval," dated July 11, 1816.
25. Thomas Jefferson, "Letter to William Johnson," dated June 12, 1823.
26. http://mohistory.org/node/87.
27. Benton, *supra*, p. 70
28. Julian P. Boyd, ed., *The Papers of Thomas Jefferson* (Princeton, NJ: Princeton University Press, 1950) et seq.; "Letter to Edward Carrington," January 16, 1787
29. Ibid.
30. This quotation appears in many places, but has never been authoritatively demonstrated to have been said by George Washington.
31. James McHenry, "Notes of the Constitutional Convention," *The American Historical Review,* vol. 11, 1906.

McHenry's notes were first published in *The American Historical Review,* vol. 11, 1906, and the anecdote on p. 618 reads: "A lady asked Dr. Franklin Well Doctor what have we got a republic or a monarchy. A republic replied the Doctor if you can keep it." When McHenry's notes were included in *The Records of the Federal Convention of 1787,* ed. Max Farrand, vol. 3, appendix A, p. 85 (1911, reprinted 1934), a footnote stated that the date this anecdote was written is uncertain.

Chapter Three

The Ayes and Nays

In this chapter, we will explore the Ayes and the Nays. Let's begin by looking at the opposition to a convention. Who are they? Why do they oppose a convention? Can their opposition be overcome, and if so, how?

To begin at the beginning, let me quote a very savvy friend of mine, who tried to discourage me from writing this book. His thesis and all encompassing conclusion was emphatic: "Forget it, Tom, nobody wants a constitutional convention."

He ticked off the list. The Congress doesn't want it. No President would want it. The Supreme Court certainly doesn't want it. Neither political party would support it. None of the people who give money to political parties and candidates want it. None of the people whose economic advantage depends on the political status quo will support a convention that could initiate a change in the rules.

None of the newspapers, radio and television stations, publishers, movie makers, and celebrities who depend on and reciprocally influence public opinion are likely to go out on a limb to support the calling of a constitutional convention.

As much as his argument sounds cynical, he certainly has a point. The Founders of our nation were well aware of the inertia that protects the status quo. The Declaration of Independence made the point quite clearly:

> Prudence indeed, will dictate that governments long established should not be changed for light and transient Causes and accordingly all Experience hath shewn, that Mankind are more disposed to suffer, while Evils are sufferable, than to right themselves by abolishing the Forms to which they are accustomed.[1]

Still, there are limits. The Tea Party and the Occupy movement evidence that on both sides of the political fence there is dissatisfaction. On both the Left and the Right there are real life Howard Beales, throwing open the window and shouting to the world, "I'm mad as hell and I'm not going to take it any longer."[2]

The shadows are alive with academic and scholarly discussion about the flaws in our system of government; barnacles on the ship of state that time and travel have suffered to accumulate.

Most importantly, to keep faith with the founders who designed our constitutional republic, we have the sacred obligation to propose and adopt those amendments which prudent and disinterested reflection on our national experience tell us are needed.

Keeping that faith requires deliberative dialog. Naked patriotism, flag waving, Fourth of July love of country and reverence for its founding documents are not enough. Fixing a dysfunctional government requires statesmanship. Patriotism born and suckled of ignorance is incompatible with statesmanship. Witness this mindless rant posted on the Internet on January 6, 2014, at 7:35 PM, at URL:www.IIIpercent.blogspot.com/2014/01/article-v-constitutional-convention.html.

Here is what it says:

> I have one position. It has not changed and it will not change. Con-con means war-war. Period. Full stop.
>
> Warning to those who think this is a good idea. You are wrong. If you manage to schedule or convene a con-con, I will be there, and I will help to burn the entire fucking place to the ground, with as many people inside as possible. That is not hyperbole. I am not kidding, even a little bit.
>
> We on the liberty side of the equation will not even get a seat at the table. And the people who would be in the room I would not let them eat . . . my . . . trash. I don't care what promises they might make going into the room, what 'limits' they promise to abide by, con-con is immediate, total war.
>
> The moment they go into the room, we burn the entire fucking block to the ground.

That blog managed to attract some sympathetic comments:

> Anonymous: January 6, 2014, 9:25 PM
>
> Wish I was closer to ground zero. I wholeheartedly agree. The scumbags entering to renegotiate my confirmed and fought for B o R don't give a shit about anyone of us in this country. They will be there for the banksters. Burn down the house . . . talking heads.
>
> NVD III

Anonymous, January 6, 2014, 10:14 PM:

> Lock the doors and gas the nest.
> Lewis III

Anonymous, January 7, 2014:

> Rather than wait until they are all in a big hall, or convention center, with security all about, instead ask where the leaders and organizers sleep tonight. A stitch in time saves nine.

The III Percent Patriots organization has a motto borrowed from Thomas Jefferson:

> "Rightful liberty is unobstructed action according to our will within limits drawn around us by the equal rights of others."[3]

Apparently Mr. Kerodin does not believe that the First Amendment right of the people peaceably to assemble draws a limit around his liberty nor does the Fifth Amendment protect from his unobstructed action the lives, liberty and property of the people he so cavalierly proposes to annihilate.

No doubt their vision of an Article V constitutional convention is a roomful of movie stars and university professors cheering a liberal agenda like that outlined by former Supreme Court Justice John Paul Stevens in his recent book, *Six Amendments: How and Why We Should Change the Constitution.*[4]

Whatever kudos Mr. Justice Stevens may earn for his superannuated productivity, the Supreme Court Reports show that he was unable even to persuade a liberal majority of his colleagues to the positions he is now espousing. The chances that the broad base of citizen opinion might take up his cudgels are slim and none.

Still, Justice Stevens' latest book does tend to stir opposition among conservatives, perhaps even among the good old boy Duck Dynasty crowd, to the whole idea of amending the constitution. The ubiquitous main stream media and its lock step support of political correctness cause many to doubt that there is a common sense middle ground in American politics.

Unfortunately, emotional attachment to the Constitution combined with ignorance of the elemental principles on which it was grounded and the actual words of the constitution itself, can lead to blind, unreasoning opposition to anything that hints of change. A near panic seems to envelop many on the Right whenever an Article V convention is mentioned. While they do not threaten to kill people or burn buildings, the John Birch Society has been a particularly aggressive and outspoken opponent of an amendatory constitutional convention.

Founded in Indianapolis in 1958 by retired manufacturer Robert Welch, Jr. and named for a Baptist Missionary who was killed by Chinese communists after World War II, the society counted some very wealthy businessmen among its founders.

Emphasizing educational activities and its conservative anti-communist agenda, the Society grew to about 100,000 members by 1961. Over the years, the John Birch Society has embraced a number of conservative causes, including withdrawal from the United Nations, and dismantling of the Federal Reserve System.

Its stated purpose is to work for less government, more responsibility and a better world. By the time Mr. Welsh died in 1985, the John Birch Society had declined in membership and influence, but its visible presence on the Internet and its financial support of the Conservative Political Action Committee (CPAC) evidence that it is still well funded.

Certainly for the last twenty-five years, the John Birch Society has been in the forefront of opposition to an Article V amendatory convention.

When a balanced budget amendment marshaled thirty-two concurrent state applications for a convention in the early 1980s, the John Birch Society responded with a campaign to stifle the effort. After successfully stalling the movement, the Society set about to persuade the state legislatures to rescind their applications. Nineteen of them did.

In the early 1990s, Utah Governor Mike Leavitt spearheaded a movement called the Conference of States that was intended to convene state delegates without an actual convention, but with the purpose of agreeing on structural changes in the relationship between the state and the federal government.

The John Birch Society labeled the effort a constitutional convention in disguise and mounted a successful campaign to defeat state resolutions in favor of it.

In 2012, a Texas businessman named Chip deMoss, working with Goldwater Institute senior fellow Nick Dranias, launched the Compact for America, an effort to persuade state legislatures to enter into an agreement to support an Article V convention on specific pre-determined conditions which would be contained in an interstate agreement known as The Compact for America.

Both deMoss and Dranias are gentlemen of a conservative bent. Their principal constitutional goal is to require fiscal responsibility in Washington, DC, a rather typical and widely approved conservative objective.

No doubt they assumed that the John Birch Society, being traditionally and notoriously conservative, would be a natural ally, and they made a vigorous outreach to enlist Birch Society support for the Compact for America.

It was not to be. Despite repeated offers to explain, defend and even alter their initiative, deMoss and Dranias were unable even to schedule an audience with the top decision makers of the Society.

Finally, based on an article printed in the John Birch publication, *The New American*, deMoss and Dranias concluded that the Society's position was:

- No matter what rules are written, and no matter that the rules are enforceable as both state and federal law, the governors at the convention will not follow them because they are bought and paid for by special interests and corporations and are actually conspiring to replace the Constitution with a new radical form of government.
- State legislators are too harried and overworked to be able to truly understand and be aware that by joining the CFA, they are actually stooges in the scheme and they are unknowingly enabling the governors to implement their plan to tear up the Constitution and replace it with a radical new form of government.
- State and federal enforcement officials are also part of the scheme to replace the Constitution and will not move to enforce the rules that the governors violate.
- Members of Congress are also part of the scheme and will readily submit the radical proposals to the state legislatures for ratification.
- The state legislators, who were too overworked to know what they are doing to begin with, will then continue their stooge roles and readily accept the new form of government schemed by the governors and Congress when it is presented to them.[5]

That is a pretty harsh indictment. It is difficult to believe that the leadership of the John Birch Society are as paranoiac as Compact for America describes.

Still, the adamant opposition of the Birch Society to any Article V initiative is hard to explain. Certainly the Birch people are not disciples of the status quo. Their website is replete with complaints about dysfunctional national government.

Among the core principles of the Birch organization is this statement:

> The John Birch Society endorses the U.S. Constitution as the foundation of our national government, and works toward educating and activating Americans to abide by the original intent of the Founding Fathers. We seek to awaken a sleeping and apathetic people concerning the designs of those who are working to destroy our constitutional Republic.[6]

It is hard to understand how an organization which "endorses the U.S. Constitution" and would "abide by the original intent of the Founding Fathers" could conclude that anyone who invokes the right to propose amendments which the Founding Fathers gave us is "working to destroy" the Republic.

REX THE RED

One explanation for the Birch Society's adamant opposition to an amendatory constitutional convention is that its leaders may have read the Tugwell constitution, and they think that any effort to promote constitutional reform is merely an extension or resurrection of that failed pipedream.

Rexford Tugwell was an academic, educated at the Wharton School of the University of Pennsylvania and at Columbia University. He helped to engineer Franklin Roosevelt's New Deal. He was the one who introduced the idea of paying farmers not to farm.

Often called "Rex the Red," Tugwell was the quintessential social planner. When named to Roosevelt's Resettlement Administration Tugwell went about moving urban slum dwellers and unemployed farmers to the suburbs until the courts declared the program unconstitutional.

In the years after World War II, Tugwell worked to create a "world constitution." Along about 1964, the Ford Foundation ponied up something like $25 million to finance the drafting of a new constitution for our country. Tugwell was the point man, and after forty drafts by over 100 academics, he announced the result: a constitution for "The New States of America."

No need to detail it here. Suffice it to say that Tugwell's constitution substitutes ten "departments" for the fifty States, and puts the federal government in charge of every aspect of everybody's life.

It would be no surprise, then, to learn that the John Birch Society and many other well-meaning American conservatives instantly relate any effort to call an Article V convention to the discredited Tugwell fizzle.

They insist that an Article V convention would be a full-blown revision of our nation's charter, a constitutional convention or "con-con" as they like to call it. Not so. Article V authorizes only a convention to propose amendments to "this constitution." "This constitution" is the one ratified by the people in 1789.

Of course, no one doubts the right of the Ford Foundation, or Mr. Tugwell and his coterie of academic dreamers, to draft a constitution. It's a free country, after all. Any group in America can get together and propose whatever they want to propose. You can do that in a free country.

But whether a proposal gets laughed at and ignored or whether it makes sense and grows legs depends on what it says and how it is understood and received by the folks who buy stock, join unions, shop at Walmart, attend church, and vote.

A constitution is written by and for the people. It is not an esoteric encryption addressed to the intelligentsia. Amendments that are written by the people will be adopted by the people, and they will not be socialist pipedreams.

The John Birch Society has been the major force in discouraging public approval of an Article V convention, and they have been quite successful in persuading conservative legislators.

A key point in their argument is always the assertion that a con con would be a 'run away' convention that would rewrite the entire 1787 document, much as the Tugwell people did.

To bolster their point and to counter those who say an Article V convention could only propose amendments to the existing constitution, opponents of the convention often cite a letter from Chief Justice Warren Burger to Phyllis Schlafly.

Here is that letter:

> June 22, 1983
> Chambers of Chief Justice Burger, Retired
>
> Dear Phyllis:
>
> I am glad to respond to your inquiry about a proposed Article V Constitutional Convention. I have been asked questions about this topic many times during my news conferences and at college meetings since I became chairman of the Commission on the Bicentennial of the U.S. Constitution, and I have repeatedly replied that such a convention would be a grand waste of time.
>
> I have also repeatedly given my opinion that there is no effective way to limit or muzzle the actions of a Constitutional Convention. The convention could make its own rules and set its own agenda. Congress might try to limit the convention to one amendment or to one issue, but there is no way to assure that the convention would obey. After a convention is convened, it will be too late to stop the convention if we don't like its agenda. The meeting in 1787 ignored the limit placed by the confederation Congress "for the sole and express purpose."
>
> With George Washington as chairman, they were able to deliberate in total secrecy, with no press coverage and no leaks. A constitutional Convention today would be a free-for-all for special interest groups, television coverage, and press speculation.
>
> Our 1787 Constitution was referred to by several of its authors as a "miracle." Whatever gain might be hoped for from a new Constitutional Convention could not be worth the risks involved. A new convention could plunge our Nation into constitutional confusion and confrontation at every turn, with no assurance that focus would be on the subjects needing attention. I have discouraged the idea of a Constitutional Convention, and I am glad to see states rescinding their previous resolutions requesting a convention. In these bicentennial years, we should be celebrating its long life, not challenging its very existence. Whatever may need repair in our Constitution can be dealt with by specific amendments.
>
> Cordially,
> (Signature)
> Warren Burger[7]

One of seven children of a Minnesota traveling salesman, Warren Burger grew up on a family farm near St. Paul. He worked his way through college and earned his law degree in night school. Ambitious and focused, he moved up through the ranks of the legal profession, until President Richard Nixon appointed him Chief Justice of the United States Supreme Court in 1969 to succeed Earl Warren.

Despite his humble beginnings, Burger was not a populist. While Nixon and others hoped he would move the Court away from the liberal track espoused by his predecessor, Burger was soon joining the Justices who had voted with Earl Warren.

He had always aspired to be a member of the intellectual elite. As Chief Justice, he achieved that goal. Thus, it was possible that a man who sprung from humble beginnings could ultimately opine that doing what the Founders of our nation enabled us to do would be a "waste of time."

He was quite right, of course, in saying that a convention makes its own rules and sets its own agenda. That is what a convention does. But when he wrote that there would be no way to stop a convention once convened, he was playing on the foolish notion that a convention can somehow change the constitution, which of course, it cannot do. Only ratification by three quarters of the states can do that.

His claim that the Philadelphia convention ignored limits set by the continental Congress simply isn't true. The 1787 convention was charged to revise the system of government, not simply to amend the Articles of Confederation. Revise means to rewrite, to do over, to rethink and that is just what they did. The role of the framers in Philadelphia was fully and persuasively defended by James Madison in Federalist #40. The claim that our Founders were unfaithful to their charge is simply not true.

Burger's fear of television and press coverage is consistent with his elitist disposition.[8] To him, a constituent assembly would be a gathering of riff-raff and trouble-makers. He much preferred government by nine cloistered men and women in the hallowed halls of the United States Supreme Court who know what is best for the people.

His letter was curious enough as an epistle by a learned man, but what was most preposterous was the last sentence. Article V clearly authorizes only specific amendments to *this* constitution. That is what Article V is for. To oppose an Article V convention and then say we can always adopt specific amendments is patently contradictory.

Still, it must be conceded that there are a great many people who insist that our government is in need of repair, but who incomprehensibly oppose the very means of repair that our Founders gave us.

One of those is Phyllis Schlafly, founder of the Eagle Forum. Now in her ninetieth year, Mrs. Schlafly came reluctantly to the ramparts of those who would defend the constitution from itself. She joins Harvard's Lawrence

Tribe, hardly her philosophical bedmate, in spraying the idea of an Article V convention with a fountain of questions.

What would the convention do? How would it work? Who would make the rules? How would delegates be chosen and by whom?

She summons up the vision of a national partisan nominating convention, with all its ruckus and disorder, and harkens back to the Democratic convention of 2012 and its summary and obviously railroaded disposition of a contested motion about putting a reference to God in the platform.

The unfounded fear of an Article V convention seems particularly to infect civic-minded people who become involved in grassroots efforts to reform our national government. It is an inexplicable phenomenon, since the Founders adopted Article V for the precise purpose of empowering the people of the states to fix the national government when necessary.

One such group was founded by radio talk show host Jackie Petru and others. Its website chronicles countless hours of efforts to prevent the calling of an Article V convention, despite forceful recitation of the need for reform of our national government.[9]

On February 19, 2009 Rick Santelli, an editor of CNBC Business News, took to the airways to rant against the Homeowners Affordability and Stability Plan, an edict by President Barack Obama designed to reduce people's mortgage payments. The gist of Santelli's opinion was that people shouldn't borrow money they can't afford to repay. He ended by suggesting that it might be time for Americans to rise up in a symbolic reenactment of the Boston Tea Party.

His video went viral, and became a rallying cry for the creation of the nationwide Tea Party movement. It organized a national demonstration on September 12, 2009 that attracted many thousands of demonstrators to Washington, DC and elsewhere. The Tea Party had an impact on the Congressional elections, especially in 2012. Still, there is no evidence that the Tea Party as an organization is interested in promoting constitutional reform, despite the conversion of Tea Party leader Mark Meckler to the cause.

So the question remains, Why do conservatives, who are vocally concerned about our dysfunctional government, who rail against unconstitutional actions by all three branches of the federal government, and who work tirelessly to recruit and organize the nation at its grassroots, either ignore efforts to call an Article V convention or actively oppose the idea?

Clearly they perceive a danger that an Article V convention might propose amendments that are contrary to conservative principles and ideals. On this, it must be conceded that, theoretically, they have a point. To the extent that the convention is a step in the process of constitutional amendment, it certainly could propose any kind of an amendment.

But opposing the convention for that reason alone is irresponsible. Just because a Congress or a Legislature might pass unpopular laws is no reason not to have a republican form of government. Political power, like atomic power or electricity has the capacity to cause damage, but properly used, these sources of energy are beneficial to mankind.

It is argued, however, that there is unnecessary risk in holding a convention because the problems of our dysfunctional national government can be alleviated in other ways. Elect different people, for example. That route, however, has lost its charm. With the help of Tea Party endorsed candidates, the Republican Party won a majority in the House of Representatives in 2010. It was a fool's errand. The Republican Party has no greater commitment to the federal constitution than does the Democratic Party. There has been no discernable improvement in the nation's capital.

We don't need a new constitution, but we do need to fix the one we have. Public confidence in a ruling intellectual elite which saunters down the Ivy Corridor from Cambridge, Massachusetts to Washington, DC, with pit stops in New Haven and New York, has worn thin. The "powers that be," the "one percent," the "mainstream media," and "Wall Street" are all short-hand ways of expressing the alienation of Main Street and the flyover space from the Alleghenies to the Rockies.

Aggressive and affirmative opposition to an Article V convention comes mostly from the political Right, which insists that the only thing wrong with our government is that the politicians don't obey the constitution as it is written.

RON PAUL

Three times a candidate for President of the United States, former Texas Congressman Ron Paul has truly established himself as an American icon. Folksy, outspoken, and personable, the retired obstetrician and gynecologist boasts of delivering more than 4,000 babies, His libertarian political philosophy appeals to young and old, and has engendered a massive following of discontent citizens.

Paul's unsuccessful 2012 Republican presidential bid has refused to melt away. Ron Paul supporters from across the country have joined forces in a political movement which calls itself the Campaign for Liberty. Ron Paul is its Chairmen and spiritual godfather.

The Campaign for Liberty's Statement of Principles echoes many of the points I am trying to make in this book. Here is an excerpt from their website:

> Americans inherit from their ancestors a glorious tradition of freedom and resistance to oppression. Our country has long been admired by the rest of the world for her great example of liberty and prosperity—a light shining in the darkness of tyranny.

> But many Americans today are frustrated. The political choices they are offered give them no real choice at all. For all their talk of "change," neither major political party as presently constituted challenges the status quo in any serious way. Neither treats the Constitution with anything but contempt. Neither offers any change in monetary policy. Neither wants to make the reductions in government that our crushing debt burden demands. Neither talks about bringing American troops home not just from Iraq, but from around the world. Our country is going bankrupt, and none of these sensible proposals are even on the table.
>
> This destructive bipartisan consensus has suffocated American political life for many years. Anyone who tries to ask fundamental questions instead of cosmetic ones is ridiculed or ignored.
>
> That is why the Campaign for Liberty was established: to highlight the neglected but commonsense principles we champion and reinsert them into the American political conversation.
>
> The U.S. Constitution is at the heart of what the Campaign for Liberty stands for, since the very least we can demand of our government is fidelity to its own governing document.[10]

The Campaign for Liberty's Statement of Principles ends with the conclusion that our country is ailing and asserts that the simple remedy includes respect for the Constitution and return to the principles of our Founding Fathers.

Given that call to action, Ron Paul's attitude toward an Article V convention is curiously contradictory. Here is what Dr. Paul has to say about the Fifth Article of the Federal Constitution in a letter which has been published on the Internet:

> Dear Friend:
>
> Thank you for expressing your concern that attempting to roll back the dangerous expansion of government power through constitutional amendment will bring about a constitutional convention. You are indeed correct that a modern constitutional convention, given today's political climate, would be dangerous to liberty by leaving us open to sudden, sweeping change in our government.
>
> I must point out, however, that initiating or passing an amendment is not calling for a constitutional convention, is not an invitation to do so, and is not nearly as dangerous. During the amendment process, we are not any more open to the dangers of a convention than at any other time. We have seen twenty-seven amendments to the Constitution without a convention being called. Amendments are the constitutional and safe way to change our form of government because the particular and limited issue addressed by an amendment requires a long, involved process to change the Constitution for very limited and specific ends. With each proposed amendment there is ample time to point out any apparent threats to liberty and warn our fellow citizens.
>
> Contrast this to the current situation where almost anything can become law if a mere, momentary majority in Congress and the current president agrees. The amendment process is the proper, constitutional way to change our

> government's power, rather than by arbitrary lawmaking or regulatory rule-making. Thank you again for your vigilance and dedication to liberty.[11]

The good doctor complains about overreaching legislation and insists that constitutional amendment is the proper way to change the government. But at the same time, he makes the ridiculous statement that the Article V amendatory convention which our forefathers wisely provided for in the Constitution of which he is so fond, would "be dangerous to liberty" and would leave us "open to sudden, sweeping change in our government"

Unhappily there is a preposterous paranoia among many conservatives and libertarians who mistakenly believe that an Article V constitutional convention would have the power to write and somehow effectuate an entirely new constitution.

They cannot have read Article V with a discerning eye. Very clearly, Article V requires ratification by three quarters of the states before any amendment becomes part of the constitution. Moreover, Article V describes the work of the convention as proposing amendments which, when ratified, become part of THIS constitution.

THIS constitution means the existing constitution, the one written in 1787 and ratified in 1789. Article V does not contemplate or authorize the drafting of an entirely new constitution.

Ron Paul speaks of the "amendment process" as being somehow distinct from an Article V convention. He is apparently referring to amendments proposed by the Congress. Surely he must realize that Congress is never going to propose amendments that would in any way restrict their current unfettered power to legislate and spend money.

The founders of whom Paul and his followers are so enamored, gave us Article V for the very purpose of controlling a dysfunctional or overweening Congress. It makes absolutely no sense to complain about Congress and at the same time oppose the means of correcting its faults.

AMEND OR NULLIFY

Publius Huldah is one of those delightfully mysterious[12] pseudonyms that make Internet browsing such a charming pastime. It's hardly a name that a Mom and Dad would saddle onto an infant child. We do know this about her: she is bright, articulate, patriotic, attractively mature, bespectacled, and passionate about the constitution.

A retired litigation attorney who now lives in Tennessee, Ms. Huldah earned a degree in philosophy with emphasis on politics and epistemology before obtaining her law degree. She now writes extensively on the U.S. Constitution, using the Federalist Papers to prove its original meaning and intent. She shows how federal judges and politicians have ignored our Constitution and replaced it with their personal opinions and beliefs. She also shows how The People can, by learning our Founding Principles themselves, restore our Constitutional Republic.

While she doesn't suffer fools gladly, Ms. Huldah's critique of the present and the recent history of our nation is very much in tune with my own, with one major exception: she abhors the Article V convention and endorses state nullification of unconstitutional federal laws.

Why does she abhor the Article V convention? It's curious. She is, after all, a daughter of the Constitution. She loves it, She praises it. She eagerly and wholeheartedly protects and defends it. Well, almost all of it. Everything but Article V. She doesn't come right out and say that Article V is a mistake. Presumably she approves of allowing the Congress to propose amendments. Otherwise, she would not be able to vote. But this convention thing, this letting the people (OMG, the PEOPLE?) come together in convention and propose amendments, what on earth were Washington, Hamilton, and Madison thinking?

Unfortunately, I am afraid that Ms. Huldah's notion of "the people" is all tied up in what she sees on television, reads in the newspapers, and learns on the Internet. A disciple of Ayn Rand, she in not inclined to agree with my confidence in the the intuitive wisdom of the great unwashed.

Still, her formula for "fixing the government" has a ring of authenticity. She quotes Thomas Jefferson, James Madison, and Alexander Hamilton to the point that human beings have a natural right to assert themselves against tyranny. That proposition has never been stated more authoritatively than in the Declaration of Independence. Governments derive their just powers from the consent of the governed. Whenever government becomes destructive of its role as the protector of the rights of the people, it is their natural, God-given right to abolish or alter it.

Publius Huldah takes that proposition to an interesting extreme. Citing the Sixth Article of the federal Constitution's requirement that all state and federal officers must take an oath to support the national constitution, she concludes that every such person has the obligation to ignore every statute, court decision, or administrative regulation which is not made pursuant to the Constitution. Presumably, she would also advocate that every American, whether a public official or not, has the right to ignore such unconstitutional laws, orders, and regulations as well.

Whatever the accuracy of that proposition, it is hardly a practical solution to the problem of legislative and judicial usurpation in Washington, DC. Indeed, nullification, as described by Jefferson and Madison is nothing more nor less than justified civil disobedience.

Martin Luther King Junior was the great apostle of civil disobedience. With courageous determination he defied unjust, irrational segregation laws. Peacefully, but forcefully, he stood his ground in the face of the armed might of the government. He went to jail, but he did not surrender. King exercised the same natural right asserted by the Founders as the right of nullification.

But the natural constituency that supported Doctor King is not likely to rally behind every protest against unconstitutional statutes and court decisions. A lonesome protest does not operate to nullify an unconstitutional act. So even if it is true that the people have the right to ignore unconstitutional acts, do such protests have the effect of rendering the offending statute or court decision a nullity? If one American protests, are all others required to do likewise?

Some have argued for a form of nullification in which the act of a State's legislature determining that a federal law is unconstitutional would immediately suspend the federal act unless three-quarters of the States' overrule the State nullification.

James Madison addressed this concept in an 1830 letter to Edward Everett. He pointed out that such a rule would permit one third of the states to dictate to the other two-thirds, saying that such a rule, "would overturn the first principle of free Government and in practice necessarily overturn the government itself."[13]

The United States of America is a unique form of government that embodies the principle of dual sovereignty. Both the state and federal governments were founded by the people of the states. The state governments didn't create the federal government and the federal government didn't create the states. The people created both governments, and the people did not empower the legislatures of either government to nullify the laws enacted by the other.

But the people did say, in Article VI of the federal constitution, that the laws of the federal government, made pursuant to the national constitution, are the supreme law of the land and the judges in every state shall be bound thereby.

Are the judges of every state bound by Congressional Acts or Federal Court decisions that are not made in pursuance of the Constitution?

I submit that Article VI means that they are not bound by unconstitutional laws. In fact the phrase "unconstitutional law" is an oxymoron. Legislation which is unconstitutional is not law at all. But if a state court declares a federal law unconstitutional, the court does not "nullify" the law. To nullify means to render null and void, literally, to "make nothing." The court's decision does not make the law nothing, The court's decision is that the unconstitutional legislation never was anything.

Ms. Huldah is adamant in her conclusion that our federal government has metastasized into an oligarchy ruled by five votes on the United States Supreme Court. Any student of constitutional history would have to agree. The public expansion of the doctrine of *stare decisis* into a virtual *carte blanche* for judicial legislation is a phenomenon that pains every person who treasures our constitution.

Abraham Lincoln was quite astute, when he noted that if public policy is to be set by the Supreme Court in deciding private litigation between individuals, the people will have ceased to be their own masters.[14] I do not read Article VI to say that the decisions of the Supreme Court are to be the supreme law of the land. Decisions of courts do not create law. They apply the law as it is written in the constitution or in the statutes lawfully adopted by the legislature.

I suppose it would be possible for people in the states to engage in a kind of semi official civil disobedience that would challenge the limits of *stare decisis*. Suppose for example that state prosecutors and judges were to decide that the United States Supreme Court's edict in the case of *Miranda v. Arizona* was simply not going to be the law of, say, South Carolina.

So imagine that South Carolina police officers stop giving people their Miranda warnings and South Carolina judges stop ruling that Miranda warnings are necessary. Very shortly, there would be a face-off between the federal and the state judges in South Carolina. The dockets of both courts would jam up; habeas corpus writs would be issued by the gross and the administration of justice would shortly become a public scandal.

The point of this avenue of discussion is merely to emphasize that nullification, whatever its historic or philosophical legitimacy, is simply not a practical remedy to defuse a federal establishment that has chosen to ignore the constitution it has been sworn to uphold.

The remedy to rein in a Supreme Court which has undertaken to be the cultural oracle of the nation is to populate the court with justices more attuned to federalism, justices who appreciate the proper role of the states as the domestic sovereigns in our constitutional system.

I submit that we cannot change the way Supreme Court Justices are chosen by some exercise of nullification. The only thing the constitution says about the Supreme Court is that the Congress shall ordain and establish one, and in Article II, Section 2, that the President shall have the power, with the consent of the Senate, to appoint the Judges, who thereafter serve during their good behavior.

Publius Huldah, the John Birch Society, and others who insist that nullification is the only proper remedy for national power-grabbing have not carried their notion to its logical conclusion. Creating a legal and political tug-of-war between the states and the federal government will not solve anything. At its worst, it could lead to secession and another civil war.

It would surely grieve the founders of our nation to awake from the dead and find that the Americans of our generation have not the wisdom or the courage to continue their inspired experiment in deliberative self government.

They gave us Article V. We have only our timidity to blame if we do not use it as intended to adopt those prudent amendments that are suggested by the experience of 230 years.

FROM THE LEFT

Opposition from the Left is very different from that of the Right. The political Left simply doesn't believe in a written constitution. It doesn't want a convention because it doesn't want the constitution of 1787 to be improved. The more quaint and archaic the constitution is perceived to be, the more acceptable are court decisions that engraft new rules of constitutional law embedded in Supreme Court decisions.

An articulate spokesman for progressives is Louis Michael Seidman, the Carmack Waterhouse Professor of Constitutional Law at Georgetown University. After graduating from Harvard Law School in 1971, Professor Seidman served as a law clerk for J. Skelly Wright of the D.C. Circuit and U.S. Supreme Court Justice Thurgood Marshall. He then was a staff attorney with the D.C. Public Defender Service until joining the Georgetown Law Center faculty in 1976.

His 2012 work, entitled *On Constitutional Disobedience* is a powerful indictment of the United States Constitution. To his credit, Professor Seidman makes no attempt to justify decisions of the United States Supreme Court as interpretations of the Constitution. On the contrary, he candidly admits that many court decisions have no basis in the words of the Constitution.

On December 30, 2012, the *New York Times* published an essay by Professor Seidman on its Op Ed page under the title "Let's Give Up On The Constitution." Seidman's comment was as revolutionary as anything Tom Paine wrote in the eighteenth century. That article accurately reveals the mindset of the intellectual elite oligarchy that rules the United States of America in the twenty-first century.

Professor Seidman believes that the biggest problem with the Constitution is the amendment process outlined in Article V. In his view, It is extremely cumbersome. In fact, he says, the American constitution is more difficult to amend than any other national constitution in the world. As a practical matter, according to the Professor, it means that under present political circumstances the Constitution is unamendable, leaving us saddled with a bunch of eighteenth-century judgments about twenty-first century problems.

In a recent interview, Professor Seidman made these observations:

> I'm not in favor of revising the Constitution. I am in favor of ignoring it. The basic argument that I make is that the United States is owned by the people presently living in it. We would not want a foreign government or the UN

> telling us how to run our country, and we should not want people long dead to tell us either. Just as it is wrong for these people to tell us what kind of country we should have, so too it would be wrong for us to dictate to future generations. Of course, the Professor does not advocate scrapping the entire scheme of governance outlined in the 1787 constitution. The Congress, the president, the courts would all continue just as they are, or perhaps just as they may evolve over time.

The Bill of Rights, he presumes, would remain in effect, not because of the words of the Constitution but rather because of a continuing national consensus in favor of free speech, freedom of the press and of religion. He doesn't seem to give much thought to the problem of what may happen when public opinion bubbles up to stifle these freedoms.

Among the curious anomalies in Professor Seidman's theory is the fact that he is critical of the status quo. For example, he calls the United States Senate "grossly malapportioned." Presumably that opinion flows from the fact that the Senate was intended to represent the states, and therefore the states have equal suffrage in that chamber, irrespective of their population.

Precisely what he would do about that problem, he does not say. How to change the composition of the Senate in a nation without a constitution, would be a challenge of the first magnitude.

Like many on the Right, Professor Seidman concedes that our nation is teetering at the edge of fiscal chaos, and that many people think that the American system of government is broken. He cites our 230-year-old constitution as the culprit calling its provisions archaic, idiosyncratic, and downright evil.

At the same time, he insists that the Presidents would be limited to two four year terms, there would still be Congress, and a Supreme Court, which he says should have the power to impose its views of political morality on the country.

In 1937, Franklin D. Roosevelt gave a Constitution Day speech in which he defined the nation's charter as a statement of aspirations rather than obligations. Professor Seidman agrees. Despite the fact that the constitution calls itself "the supreme law of the land," Seidman and Roosevelt deny that its provisions are obligatory. What exactly the ceremony of oath-taking which inaugurates each new public official is supposed to mean or accomplish, the good professor does not address.

One of the Professor's main arguments echoes the view of Thomas Jefferson and Thomas Paine, to the point that life is for the living; that every generation has the right to determine its own rules, and none has the authority to bind those who come after. Nor should anyone be bound by rules made before they were born by people no longer living.

It's an interesting romantic and theoretical notion. Paine liked to talk about a lone human on an island, whose freedom is complete and unbounded.

Of course, the fellow on the island isn't likely to have a lot of fun, other than a sort of Ayn Randish sense of accomplishment when he builds himself a tree hut. He will never know love, the true essence of human life, and in due course, he will be gone, without a trace.

The truth is that no human being is completely without debt to his or her forbears. From the cradle to the coffin, we use the knowledge, skill and accomplishments of those who have gone before us, and only a person devoid of all virtue and morality can be indifferent to the duties owed to his posterity.

Seidman speaks for many on the left who denigrate the wisdom of our national founders by branding them "slave owning white men," as if slave owning white men could not possibly have any useful understanding of the value of democracy or the danger of tyranny.

I can only envision the idiocy of ridiculing George Washington's masterful Farewell Address because the "the stupid old fool was wearing wooden dentures."

George Washington's admonition that the Constitution is sacredly obligatory on all until changed by the explicit and authoritative act of the whole people would not have been more accurate and useful if articulated through SR-IVOCAP dentures.

The founders did not see the constitution as the voice of generations past echoing from the grave. They saw it as the expression of the consent of the governed—the governed being the people living in the here and now.

That consent is expressed in the simple fact that the current generation accepts and obeys the constitution as it is written without exercising their right to amend it. Seidman and his colleagues insist, no doubt, that the people living today do not have the practical ability to amend the constitution, and therefore their consent to be governed by it cannot be inferred from their acquiescence.

To a great extent, what Professors Seidman, Levinson, and others perceive as the practical impossibility of amending the constitution is a self-imposed paralysis; the product of timidity, suspicion, cynicism, and elitism. To a legal and academic community enthralled with its ownership of the nuances of constitutional interpretation, the folksy notion of a constitution which says what it means and means what it says is a loathsome anathema.

Let's face it, people who think it's a good idea to empower nine lifetime political appointees to dictate the cultural norms of 308 million people are not likely to trust what six thousand citizen-jurors from every community in the nation might want to see written into the constitution.

THE BIG LIE

Whatever the merits of his other arguments, Seidman's assertion that the convention of 1787 disobeyed its instruction is flat out wrong. In the first place, the Philadelphia assembly, as we have seen, was not originally called by Congress but was organized at the behest of the men who met in Annapolis in 1786 at the "Meeting of Commissioners to Remedy Defects of the Federal Government."

Those twelve men recommended to their respective legislatures, not only that a convention of all the states meet in Philadelphia in May of 1787, but that it have "more enlarged powers" because of "facts and circumstances" rendering "the situation of the United States delicate and critical." They asked that the delegates be told to "take into consideration the situation of the United States" and "to devise such other and further provisions as shall appear to them necessary to render the Constitution of the federal government adequate to the exigencies of the Union."

The resolution of the Congress confirming their decision to meet in Philadelphia specified that they were to REVISE the Articles of Confederation, not to amend them, as so often erroneously recited by opponents of the convention. "Revise" means to rewrite, to do over, to reconsider, and that is what the Founders did.

There is another word in the Congressional call for the 1787 convention that opponents of an Article V convention seem to ignore. Let's look at the resolution again:

> Resolved that in the opinion of Congress it is expedient that on the second Monday in May next a Convention of delegates who shall have been appointed by the several states be held at Philadelphia for the sole and express purpose of *revising* the Articles of Confederation and reporting to Congress and the several legislatures such alterations and provisions therein as shall when agreed to in Congress and confirmed by the states render the federal *constitution* adequate to the exigencies of Government & the preservation of the Union.[15]

The Founders knew what a constitution is. They had all been involved in drafting and adopting constitutions in their home states. They knew that a constitution is a charter of government, in which the sovereign people give their consent to be governed in a certain way by officials chosen in a certain way. They also knew that the Articles of Confederation were not a constitution. The Articles were a "firm league of friendship" among thirteen sovereign states. The Articles of Confederation were simply a treaty. It was an agreement among governments, not an agreement of the people.

The Philadelphia convention was expected to rewrite the arrangement among the thirteen states in such a way as to be a true constitution. The preamble of the Articles of Confederation begins with "we the undersigned

Delegates of the States." It then says that the name of the confederation is "The United States of America."

As we have seen, In 1787 the "United States of America" was not a nation. It had no "people." It had no citizens. Only the individual states had people, or citizens.

The preamble of the constitution written in Philadelphia begins with these words, "We the people of the United States, in order to form a more perfect union . . ."

The delegates were not in Philadelphia to represent the governments of the thirteen states, they were there to act on behalf of the people of the thirteen states.

It is significant that the preamble ends with the words "ordain and establish this constitution for the United States of America." They were saying that the entity known as the United States of America was now to have a constitution, that is a charter from the people rather than a mere agreement among governments.

The 1787 constitution created a nation. It is a unique kind of a nation, in which the people have dual citizenship. They are citizens of the states and they are citizens of the nation. The nation known as "The United States of America" was created by the people of the several states. It can only be changed by the people of the several states. It follows that an Article V convention is a convention of the people of the states.

There is another argument that needs to be made on this subject. The attendees at the Philadelphia convention included some of the most distinguished and knowledgeable leaders of the day: George Washington, Benjamin Franklin, James Madison, Alexander Hamilton among them. They were good citizens and true patriots. It is obvious that they were of the opinion that it was right and proper for them to do what they did. To insist that the convention was a rogue gathering that ignored its rightful obligation is to suggest that these good men were consciously disregarding their mission.

Finally, it bears repeating that James Madison authoritatively established, in Federalist #40, that the Convention did what it was expected to do. The learned Professor of Law ought to have addressed and attempted to refute that significant essay.

Despite the fact that Professor Seidman makes the same erroneous claim about the intended purpose of the 1787 convention as does John Birch Society editor Joseph Wolverton, he comes from a very different perspective than that of the John Birch Society's writer. Wolverton and his colleagues are unhappy about the way our government works. They believe that the Constitution is being ignored in Washington, DC. They want the Constitution to be obeyed according to its plain meaning, and they believe that such faithful fulfillment of the oaths taken by our nation's elected officials will essentially solve all of our problems.

Seidman and his ilk however, simply think that we don't need a written constitution. England doesn't have one. England has tradition, and, in the view of Professor Seidman, tradition is good enough. If Seidman has any complaints about how things are done in Washington, DC and around the country, his preferred solution is simply more legislation and more activist Supreme Court decisions.

In short, opposition to an Article V convention from the Left essentially maintains that we don't need an amendatory convention because we don't need a written constitution.

James Madison famously observed that if men were angels, no government would be necessary. Perhaps it is also true that if all men were graduates of the Harvard Law School, no constitution would be necessary, either.

The truth is that we are neither angels nor Harvard graduates. We are a nation of people whose forebears believed that a written constitution is the only rational alternative to the bloody historic cycle that rotates between anarchy to dictatorship. Being the product of imperfect human beings, our system of government is not, and never will be perfect. But we must keep trying to make it better. To abandon the magnificent experiment after 230 years would be tragic madness.

NOTES

1. The Declaration of Independence, Second Continental Congress, July 4, 1776.
2. Howard Beale was a deranged television personality in Paddy Chayefsky's 1976 film, *Network*.
3. Thomas Jefferson, "Letter to Isaac H. Tiffany," 1819.
4. John Paul Stevens, *Six Amendments: How and Why We Should Change the Constitution,*(New York: Little Brown and Company, 2014).
5. http://www.compactforamerica.org/wp-content/uploads/CFA-A-message-to-JBS-members.pdf.
6. http://www.jbs.org/about-jbs/core-principles.
7. http://www.eagleforum.org/topics/concon/pdf/WarrenBurger-letter.pdf.
8. Burger is reputed to have barred from the courtroom an attorney who appeared in court wearing a dress shirt with a button down collar.
9. http://www.sweetliberty.org.
10. http://www.campaignforliberty.org/about/.
11. http://targetfreedom.com/bills-in-congress/ron-paul-on-constitutional-convention.
12. http://publiushuldah.wordpress.com/about/.
13. James Madison, "Letter to Edward Everett," *supra*.
14. Abraham Lincoln, "First Inaugural Address."
15. http://avalon.law.yale.edu/18th_century/const04.asp.

Chapter Four

Reasoning Together

As we have seen, the far Left and the far Right are in total agreement on three important points. They both agree that public officials in the national government routinely violate the oaths they have taken to support and defend the Constitution of the United States. They also agree that the national government, as it is currently being operated, is dysfunctional and desperately needs to be improved. Finally, at the extremes of both Left and Right there is total and adamant opposition to a convention as authorized by Article V of the United States Constitution. Now or ever.

There are, however, a great many people in the broad middle of the political spectrum who favor the calling of a convention, or who would support the idea, given enough information about it. Typically, these people immediately ask, "What would the convention do?" Pragmatism, being the unofficial state religion in our country, we go immediately to the bottom line, and measure the need by the value of the outcome.

The frantic opposition from the fringes, who insist that a convention might "run away" and propose all sorts of undesirable things, exacerbates the doubts of the unpersuaded. As a consequence, supporters of constitutional reform are confronted with the double challenge of proposing an amendment that is popular and doing it in a way that allays fears that a convention might do more than propose their popular amendment.

A horrible example of the kind of almost paranoiac fear of a "run away" convention can be seen in the Indiana Senate's Enrolled Act 234, which establishes a system of "paired" delegates to an Article V convention and disqualifies any delegate or alternate who disobeys the instructions of the legislature.

In fact, the Enrolled Act seems to impose the possibility of criminal prosecution of a delegate who dares to exercise independent judgment during the convention.

The idea of prosecuting a delegate for voting contrary to instructions runs headlong into collision with the whole purpose and definition of an Article V convention. A convention is a deliberative assembly. The essential object of a convention is to provide a means for people to reason together, to discuss, debate and deliberate.

Telling a convention delegate not to deliberate is like giving a youngster a ticket to Disney World, then punishing him for riding the roller coaster. Telling people not to pray in church, or not to cheer at a football game is nonsense. Deliberating is what people do at conventions. It is what conventions are for.

One of those who support the effort to handcuff convention delegates to the instructions of state legislatures is Nick Dranias, a senior fellow at the Goldwater Institute in Arizona. Dranias holds the Clarence J. and Katherine P. Duncan Chair for constitutional government and is director of the Joseph and Dorothy Donnelly Moller Center for Constitutional Government at the Institute. A cum laude graduate of Boston University, Dranias earned his law degree from Loyola University in Chicago, where he served on the Law Review and excelled in Moot Court competition.

Along with Texas business executive Chip deMoss, Dranias is a moving force in the Compact for America. Drafted by Dranias, the compact plans to bind its signatories to seek an Article V convention for the sole and exclusive purpose of proposing a specific balanced budget amendment to the United States Constitution.

According to its website, the Compact for America uses an agreement among the states to generate a "turn key" approach to originating its "powerful" Balanced Budget Amendment (BBA). The Compact organizes its member states to apply to Congress for a convention to propose the BBA under Article V of the U.S. Constitution and it designates and instructs member state delegates to advance only the BBA.

It specifies the convention location, agenda, rules, and committee structure. It limits the convention to a single twenty-four hour session devoted to an up or down vote on the BBA. It prohibits any other agenda and bars every member state from ratifying anything that might be proposed by the convention other than the BBA. Then, assuming that it is approved by the convention and referred by Congress to the states for ratification, it presumes to ratify the amendment in advance.

The Compact for America also ensures that the convention will be organized only if thirty-eight states join the compact and only if Congress calls the convention in accordance with the Compact. This would make sure that nothing happens until both ratification can be achieved without further legislative action and the convention logistics set out in the Compact have obtained the status of both state and federal law and are guaranteed under the Contracts Clause of the United States Constitution and under current U.S. Supreme Court precedent.

WHAT IT SAYS

Now let's take a look at the pre-packaged constitutional amendment which Compact for America wants approved in twenty-four hours with no questions asked and no debate. Here it is:

> *The Balanced Budget Amendment*
>
> Section 1. Total outlays of the government of the United States shall not exceed total receipts of the government of the United States at any point in time unless the excess of outlays over receipts is financed exclusively by debt issued in strict conformity with this article.
>
> Section 2. Outstanding debt shall not exceed authorized debt, which initially shall be an amount equal to 105 percent of the outstanding debt on the effective date of this article. Authorized debt shall not be increased above its aforesaid initial amount unless such increase is first approved by the legislatures of the several states as provided in Section 3.
>
> Section 3. From time to time, Congress may increase authorized debt to an amount in excess of its initial amount set by Section 2 only if it first publicly refers to the legislatures of the several states an unconditional, single subject measure proposing the amount of such increase, in such form as provided by law, and the measure is thereafter publicly and unconditionally approved by a simple majority of the legislatures of the several states, in such form as provided respectively by state law; provided that no inducement requiring an expenditure or tax levy shall be demanded, offered or accepted as a quid pro quo for such approval. If such approval is not obtained within sixty (60) calendar days after referral then the measure shall be deemed disapproved and the authorized debt shall thereby remain unchanged.
>
> Section 4. Whenever the outstanding debt exceeds 98 percent of the debt limit set by Section 2, the President shall enforce said limit by publicly designating specific expenditures for impoundment in an amount sufficient to ensure outstanding debt shall not exceed the authorized debt. Said impoundment shall become effective thirty (30) days thereafter, unless Congress first designates an alternate impoundment of the same or greater amount by concurrent resolution, which shall become immediately effective. The failure of the President to designate or enforce the required impoundment is an impeachable misdemeanor. Any purported issuance or incurrence of any debt in excess of the debt limit set by Section 2 is void.
>
> Section 5. No bill that provides for a new or increased general revenue tax shall become law unless approved by a two-thirds roll call vote of the whole number of each House of Congress. However, this requirement shall not apply to any bill that provides for a new end user sales tax which would completely

> replace every existing income tax levied by the government of the United States; or for the reduction or elimination of an exemption, deduction, or credit allowed under an existing general revenue tax.
>
> Section 6. For purposes of this article, "debt" means any obligation backed by the full faith and credit of the government of the United States; "outstanding debt" means all debt held in any account and by any entity at a given point in time; "authorized debt" means the maximum total amount of debt that may be lawfully issued and outstanding at any single point in time under this article; "total outlays of the government of the United States" means all expenditures of the government of the United States from any source; "total receipts of the government of the United States" means all tax receipts and other income of the government of the United States, excluding proceeds from its issuance or incurrence of debt or any type of liability; "impoundment" means a proposal not to spend all or part of a sum of money appropriated by Congress; and "general revenue tax" means any income tax, sales tax, or value-added tax levied by the government of the United States excluding imposts and duties.
>
> Section 7. This article is immediately operative upon ratification, self-enforcing, and Congress may enact conforming legislation to facilitate enforcement.

Among the drawbacks associated with constitutional amendments that are drafted by one person, whether on a kitchen table or in an academic library, is the fact that they have not been exposed to the sanitizing fire of the Devil's Advocate. So let's take a careful look at what CFA proposes.

The first fact that jumps out is that the Balanced Budget Amendment proposal—we'll call it the BBA— involves the state legislatures directly in the process of federal legislation. It requires the approval of a majority of the state legislatures to increase the federal debt limit. Interestingly, Section 3 also contains a caveat forbidding the offer of, or demand for, any inducement requiring an expenditure or tax levy as a quid pro quo for state legislative approval.

So let's think about that for a moment. We are all familiar with the present abominable process of raising the debt ceiling. An exercise in pure politics, it involves all of the horse-trading, pork-barreling, lobby-laden, deadline-threatening give and take that goes into every piece of major legislation in Washington, DC.

What kind of naiveté would suppose it possible to invite several thousand state legislators to that party and expect them to behave themselves?

There is a built-in constituency for raising the debt ceiling. It is the same constituency that supports and motivates increased deficit spending. It encompasses every sort of special pleader from the military-industrial complex to the vast throng of entitlement recipients. To suppose that state legislators will be immune from inducements or that inducements can be effectively banned in the constitution is to suppose what never was nor ever can be.

Taxing and spending are the particular jurisdiction and responsibility of legislative bodies. Whether to tax or spend or save or borrow are all "what to do" decisions. Constitutions should not dictate "what to do" decisions. Constitutions deal with the Who and the How of government, not the What or the When.

A further thought: To call this a Balanced Budget Amendment is a misnomer. This proposal does not require a balanced budget. It simply introduces an additional step to increase the national debt. The State of California's debt of almost half a trillion dollars increases by a thousand dollars every five seconds. Illinois is $154 billion in the red. New York owes more than a third of a trillion. State legislators, it would seem, are not necessarily frugal stewards of the public purse.

What to do about burgeoning public debt is not a conundrum likely to be solved without serious discussion and debate. There are alternatives that need to be examined in a deliberative setting. The constitution deals with systemic directives. Merely spreading the blame or diluting and diffusing the responsibility would not prevent deficit spending. In fact that strategy would make the status quo more intractable and an actual remedy more difficult to achieve. Trying to impose fiscal responsibility by amending the constitution requires a great deal of deliberation and debate. It will involve some tough choices. There are no simple or easy ways to assure prudent decision-making in legislative bodies. There will always be external pressures on elected officials who have the power to spend the public's money.

Balancing the budget is, per se, an artificial process. A budget, by definition, is an estimate of revenues and expenses. Balancing estimates is simply a matter of opinion, hardly a basis for constitutional requirement. Balancing actual income and outgo is another matter, although factually, it depends on the integrity and accuracy of the bookkeeper.

Crafting constitutional language that prevents the government from going into debt, automatically, while leaving the sovereign entity the capacity to deal with any catastrophic threat to the common weal is a dicey business. It will take a lot of thought and a great deal of deliberation.

The whole point of this book is to advocate the creation of a permanent constitutional convention that will deal with the structure of government, so that, to the extent possible, the process of governing will be more nearly directed toward the common good.

The Compact for America website also features a counting clock that marks the minutes before a proposed deadline of July 4, 2014. Elsewhere it asserts that the Compact for America enables its balanced budget amendment to be proposed and ratified in ten months time. That seems a little too optimistic. Constitutional reform is no sport for the short-winded.

CONVENTION OF STATES

The Convention of States is another initiative that deserves attention. Its stellar leadership includes Michael Farris, who is the chancellor of Patrick Henry College and chairman of the Home School Legal Defense Association. He was the founding president of each organization. During his career as a constitutional appellate litigator, he has served as lead counsel in the United States Supreme Court, eight federal circuit courts, and the appellate courts of thirteen states.

Farris has been well-known on Capitol Hill for over thirty years and is widely respected for his leadership in the defense of homeschooling, religious freedom, and the preservation of American sovereignty. A prolific author, Farris has been recognized with numerous awards, including the Salvatori Prize for American Citizenship by the Heritage Foundation and as one of the "Top 100 Faces in Education for the 20th Century" by *Education Week* magazine.

Doctor Farris received his BA in political science from Western Washington University. He later went on to earn his JD from Gonzaga University School of Law, and his LLM in public international law from the University of London.

Associated with Mike Farris is a man familiar to many in the Tea Party movement. His name is Mark Meckler and he is the founder and president of Citizens for Self-Governance (CSG), an organization created to support grassroots activism in taking power from Washington, DC, and returning it to its rightful owners, the citizens of the United States. Mr. Meckler is the co-founder and former National Coordinator for the Tea Party Patriots, the largest tea party organization in the nation. He left the organization in February 2012 and founded CSG to expand the self-governance movement beyond the partisan divide.

Mr. Meckler graduated from San Diego State University–California State University with his BA in English literature. He later received his JD from University of the Pacific, McGeorge School of Law, where he graduated with honors.

The Convention of States project proceeds on a basis that is somewhat different from other Article V initiatives. Realizing that a single proposed amendment is a limiting factor, and wanting to enlist support from a number of Article V groups, Convention of States adopted an inclusive defining purpose. Here is what their website says:

> Two goals separate our plan from all other Article V organizations:
>
> 1. We want to call a convention for a particular subject rather than a particular amendment. Instead of calling a convention for a balanced budget

amendment (though we are entirely supportive of such an amendment), we want to call a convention for the purpose of limiting the power and jurisdiction of the federal government.

2. We believe the grassroots is the key to calling a successful convention. The goal is to build a political operation in a minimum of forty states, getting 100 people to volunteer in at least 75 percent of the state's legislative districts. We believe this is very doable. Only through the support of the American people will this project have a chance to succeed.

Our Solution is Big Enough to Solve the Problem. Rather than calling a convention for a specific amendment, Citizens for Self-Governance (CSG) has launched the Convention of the States Project to urge state legislatures to properly use Article V to call a convention for a particular subject—reducing the power of Washington, D.C. It is important to note that a convention for an individual amendment (e.g., a Balanced Budget Amendment) would be limited to that single idea. Requiring a balanced budget is a great idea that CSG fully supports. Congress, however, could comply with a Balanced Budget Amendment by simply raising taxes. We need spending restraints as well. We need restraints on taxation. We need prohibitions against improper federal regulation. We need to stop unfunded mandates.

A convention of states needs to be called to ensure that we are able to debate and impose a complete package of restraints on the misuse of power by all branches of the federal government. [1]

Meckler and Farris are both charismatic men who have had experience in organizing and inspiring grassroots efforts. Unlike so many other Article V advocates, Convention of States is not content merely to present its ideas to state legislators. Instead, they have put together a populist organization. Its goal is to create a structured volunteer organization that will help to lobby state legislatures to adopt convention petitions in the format they are advocating. From this structured organization, they plan to muster at least 25 people to attend legislative hearings whenever their proposed Article V resolutions are being considered. This is precisely the strategy that the John Birch Society has used so successfully to defeat convention petitions.

Their website is upbeat and attractive. Their follow-up with volunteers and contributors is energetic and persistent. They appear to be well financed. Also on the plus side is the fact that Convention of the States trumpets a real convention, one that will set its own agenda and make its own rules. This brings it closer to the Founders understanding of the nature of conventions, and indicates that they expect some real give and take when the convention is called to order. That factor, however will play into the John Birch cry that the convention might "run away."

Here is the standard form of resolution that COS seeks to have adopted in at least thirty-four state legislatures:

Whereas, the Founders of our Constitution empowered State Legislators to be guardians of liberty against future abuses of power by the federal government, and

Whereas, the federal government has created a crushing national debt through improper and imprudent spending, and

Whereas, the federal government has invaded the legitimate roles of the states through the manipulative process of federal mandates, most of which are unfunded to a great extent, and

Whereas, the federal government has ceased to live under a proper interpretation of the Constitution of the United States, and

Whereas, it is the solemn duty of the States to protect the liberty of our people—particularly for the generations to come—by proposing Amendments to the Constitution of the United States through a Convention of the States under Article V for the purpose of restraining these and related abuses of power,

Be it therefore resolved by the legislature of the State of ______:

Section 1. The legislature of the State of ______ hereby applies to Congress, under the provisions of Article V of the Constitution of the United States, for the calling of a convention of the states limited to proposing amendments to the Constitution of the United States that impose fiscal restraints on the federal government, limit the power and jurisdiction of the federal government, and limit the terms of office for its officials and for members of Congress.

Section 2. The secretary of state is hereby directed to transmit copies of this application to the President and Secretary of the United States Senate and to the Speaker and Clerk of the United States House of Representatives, and copies to the members of the said Senate and House of Representatives from this State; also to transmit copies hereof to the presiding officers of each of the legislative houses in the several States, requesting their cooperation.

Section 3. This application constitutes a continuing application in accordance with Article V of the Constitution of the United States until the legislatures of at least two-thirds of the several states have made applications on the same subject.[2]

There is a downside, however. Their goal of reining in the federal government is described in terms that would have little appeal to citizens whose politics are left of center. There is no mention of the Citizens United case or of corporate lobbying, no trumpeted concern for government invasion of citizen privacy, no talk of reining in Presidential war powers.

The fact that the effort is targeted to forty of the fifty states also suggests that the leadership may have an agenda component in mind, which, although not yet specific, will have a decided philosophic bent to the right.

Meckler and Farris are both fine public speakers and they have been out on the stump explaining their plans and generating support from organizations such as ALEC, the American Legislative Exchange Council. That is a mixed blessing. ALEC is an organization that brings business leaders and legislators together to discuss problems and examine public policy options. It is perceived by many Democrats as a Republican, pro-business, lobbying organization.

To be successful, an Article V convention must be scrupulously non-partisan. The goal of achieving national consensus must be always in mind. Strategizing on the basis of red states and blue states is a fool's mission that will doom any effort to achieve constitutional reform.

LEVIN AND LIBERTY

This brings us to a consideration of Mark Levin, the brilliant, controversial, conservative talk show host who has created a national buzz with his best-selling book, *The Liberty Amendments*.

Born in 1957, Mark Levin, (he pronounces it "LeVIN") roared through high school in three years, and then college in two, graduating summa cum laude from Temple University—wearing his Phi Beta Kappa pin—at the age of nineteen. Three years later he received his JD degree from Temple University's Beasley School of Law. Active in politics, Levin served in various capacities during the Reagan administration, including a stint as Chief of Staff for Attorney General Edwin Meese. He received the Ronald Reagan Award from the American Conservative Union in 2001.

So there's no question of where Mark Levin is coming from. If he has given the Article V cause a boost, he has also given it an aura. While more people know about the need for a convention, it is also true that more people think the convention is a conservative initiative.

Let's see how true that is. The first of Levin's amendments would establish term limits for Members of Congress. It simply provides that no person may serve more than twelve years as a Member of Congress, whether such service is exclusively in the House or the Senate or combined in both.

That would affect Republicans and Democrats alike. There may be some arguments against term limits, and we will talk about that later in these pages, but for now, it is enough to observe that term limits is a non-partisan reform.

Levin's second proposed amendment would repeal the seventeenth amendment, returning the power to appoint Senators to the state legislatures. This is somewhat neutral, with a slight tilt to the right. The whole idea of a Senate in which every state, regardless of its population has an equal vote, is, of course, not very popular with large, heavily populated states.

A twelve year term limit for Supreme Court Justices is Levin's third suggestion. Again, this affects liberals and conservatives equally, but Levin includes a novel provision permitting override of Supreme Court decisions by the Congress or the state legislatures. At first blush it would appeal to liberals who are concerned about the Citizens United decision, but Levin also limits overrides to twenty-four months after the court decision so his amendment would not affect Citizens United.

Levin's fourth suggestion requires Congress to adopt an annual budget and imposes a five percent across the board reduction in expenditures for failure to do so. It consists of eight sections and might be opposed by liberals who view any restriction on government spending with a jaundiced eye.

His fifth proposal limits income taxes to a maximum of 15 percent. This would be strongly opposed by most Democrats, who tend to favor steeply graduated tax rates.

Number six would phase out federal departments and agencies not reauthorized every three years. This is another idea that would get thumbs down from the left side of the aisle. His seventh suggestion, declaring limits to the Interstate Commerce clause would likewise get booed from the left.

The eighth would protect property owners from collateral taking by the government, a proposal likely to appeal to almost everyone.

Levin's ninth amendment would grant the states the authority to adopt amendments to the federal constitution by concurrent resolutions of two-thirds of the state legislatures, making it much easier to amend the U.S. Constitution. This idea would be opposed by just about everybody.

Number ten legalizes nullification of Congressional enactments by state legislatures. Only a small minority of conservatives would support that idea, and no one from the left would favor it.

Levin's eleventh proposal is designed to protect the vote. It would appeal to conservatives who believe that there is much voter fraud in big cities. It would not appeal to conservatives who believe that voting is a function that belongs within the jurisdiction of the states, and, of course, those who seek to herd the least interested non voters to the polls will oppose it.

There is no doubt that Mark Levin has contributed to the dialog about amending the constitution. He has issued a wake-up call to all Americans concerned about the malaise of our national government, and he has confronted the issue of national versus state sovereignty.

Mark Levin is clearly a brilliant man. His would be a valuable voice in a constitutional convention. Unhappily in this day of mass communication there is both an upside and a downside to celebrity. Being a celebrated author, Levin's thoughts on the subject of constitutional reform were instantly picked up by news media. Hannity invited him to share the microphone. Huckabee had him on. He made a splash. Limbaugh talked to him on the air.

These appearances on Fox News plus Levin's image as a conservative commentator sparked a visceral response from many on the left that caused them to conclude that an Article V convention is a conservative initiative.

BOB SCHULTZ

A graduate engineer with a master's in business administration, Robert L. Schultz studied public administration at the State University of New York. After being honorably discharged from the U.S. Air Force in 1959, Schultz had a varied career in industry and government, including a stint on Wall Street. A man of many talents, he founded a consulting firm and hosted a radio talk show in Albany.

Although not an attorney, he has spent more time in court than many. As a kind of self-styled government watchdog, he has been a litigant in ninety-nine state court cases and fifteen cases in federal courts. Of particular interest to Bob Schultz are the last ten words of the First Amendment to the United States Constitution. They affirm that the Congress shall make no law respecting the right of the people peaceably to assemble, and to petition the Government for a redress of grievances.

His efforts to induce the President, the Congress and the Courts to respond to petitions for redress of grievances are legendary. At one point he went on a hunger strike, consuming nothing but water, in an effort to induce the federal government to answer his petition. At another point, under the slogan "No answer, no taxes" he wrote the IRS to say that until they addressed his concerns, he would withhold payment of taxes. Not a very effective strategy, as it turned out.

Still, that episode revealed how draconian the national government can be when challenged. The Internal Revenue Service actually sued Schultz to require him to disclose the names of all persons he had urged to cooperate in his tax protest. George Orwell would have been proud to hear of that episode.

In 2008, Schultz organized a meeting at Jekyll Island that called for a gathering the following year to be known as the Continental Congress of 2009. One hundred sixteen delegates representing forty-eight of the fifty states attended the Congress and adopted a number of resolutions protesting government actions claimed to violate the federal constitution. Schultz still actively maintains a website.

I found this entry there of particular interest:

> At 9 AM on Saturday, October 8, I was tuned into CNN, broadcasting from Atlanta. The Host was interviewing three young people who had participated in "Occupy Atlanta" the day before. One was a 26 year old female veteran back from the hostilities in Iraq and Afghanistan and enrolled in College. The other two were males in their 20s who were employed. The host asked what the Occupy movement was all about. The young people said, "We want to fix the system."
>
> The host asked how the system could be fixed. The young people struggled to find an answer but had none. Eventually they suggested more people should vote.

> I turned to Judy, my wife, saying, "That's it. I'm going down there. These folks need to know about the Constitution and how it can solve their grievances." Four hours later, we were in New York City. I had a thought to find a meeting room somewhere near to the protests so I could talk about Liberty and the Constitution to whomever might come. Research uncovered a new community center two blocks away called "Charlotte's Place." We were able to make contact with and then meet with the director in between visits to the Park. He agreed to give us time to meet there with interested people.
>
> As we walked among the protestors, we observed many who were clean-cut, bright eyed as they moved throughout the crowd open to exchanging ideas with strangers.
>
> I noticed a table with a homemade sign, "INFO." I approached and asked, "How can I conduct a teach-in on the State and Federal Constitutions? The young man said, "Start a Working Group." I asked, "How do I do that." He said, "Announce it." I asked, "How?" He said, "Get up on a bench and yell, 'Mic Check.' That will get the attention of the People."
>
> I did just that. The People turned their attention to me and began to repeat, in waves, every few words I said. I announced I was starting a Constitution Working Group, that the Constitution can be used to control the Bankers, the Corporations and the Politicians, end undeclared wars, end Bailouts, end the Fed and end our debt-based, fiat currency. Each part of the message was repeated two or three times as the crowds carried the words and energy back to others farther away. I announced the first meeting of the State and Federal Constitution Working Group would be at 6 PM on the steps at the east end of the Plaza.
>
> Cheers were heard and People raised both hands, pointing all their (wiggling) fingers upwards. I learned later that was a hand signal expressing approval.[3]

I found this story of particular interest, because it has seemed to me that many of the young people who flocked to the Occupy movement were in search of some method to "petition for redress of grievances" and, given an opportunity to avail themselves of constitutional avenues of redress, they would join with other activist groups. Bob Schultz is probably light years to the right of the Wall Street protesters in his political views, but in terms of challenging the status quo, he has demonstrated courage that should make him a hero to the Occupiers.

OTHER VOICES

Certainly, the push for constitutional reform is not coming exclusively from the right. A number of recognized writers and scholars have weighed in on the need for amendments of one kind or another.

Sanford Levinson, a professor of law and government at the University of Texas in Austin, has written extensively and critically about the Constitution of 1787. Professor Levinson ticks off a number of shortcoming and anachronisms in the nation's charter, and then adds that its greatest fault is Article V, and the difficult road it defines for proposing and adopting constitutional amendments.

Unlike many on the Right, Professor Levinson welcomes the idea of an Article V convention and believes that the nation would benefit from an open ended review of its supreme law. He points to Theodore Roosevelt and Woodrow Wilson, two Presidents associated with the progressive era in American politics, who would have welcomed an Article V constitutional convention. In Levinson's view the only thing a "run away" convention might do is to distance itself from some of the unpopular constitutional provisions, like the Electoral College.

Professor Levinson, like Justice John Paul Stevens, would favor a constitutional amendment either eliminating the second Amendment, or somehow circumscribing it.

No doubt many people who are supporters of the second amendment wonder why anyone who is of like mind would advocate a convention that could propose an amendment to abolish it, or, even more inconsistently, welcome opponents of the second amendment to the Article V table?

The explanation is quite simple. There are all sorts of hot button issues strewn across the political landscape. Those buttons are hot because of the strength of feelings on both sides. They are not the kind of issues likely to be addressed or resolved by a convention. Constitutional amendments require a super majority of thirty-eight state ratifications.

The second amendment has the inertia of the status quo behind it. Unless three quarters of the states can agree, there will be no change in it. That said, it is no good reason not to have a convention because we may disagree with what some people would like it to do. By definition, a convention is a forum for compromise. Only amendments that can be supported by both second amendment camps have a chance of being adopted.

Another important progressive voice is that of Harvard Law School Professor Lawrence Lessig. Author of seven books and founding sponsor of several grassroots organizations aimed particularly at the dominance of corporate money in the political arena, Lessig advocates an Article V convention as the only practical way to rein in what he has described at the "gift economy" in Washington, DC.

At the core, many liberals and conservatives agree on the need for systemic changes that will alter the milieu in the nation's capital. Often they complain of the same problem, but, seeing it in different perspectives, they support different solutions.

A little sojourn into the progressive territory on the World Wide Web reveals some opinions which might well have emanated from Fox News. Here are a few samples:

Movetoamend.org:

> Our perspective is that no "artificial entities"—non human beings—should have rights spelled out under the Constitution. This includes unions and non-profit corporations.
>
> Rights do not come from government, we have them because of the very fact that we are alive—they are inalienable. Given that, government does not actually have authority to grant rights to entities created by law. Certain powers and privileges may be needed and desired for certain entities over others, but not constitutional rights.[4]

Here is another interesting quote from Movetoamend.org:

> Our use of the term "democracy" is shorthand for what is technically our political syste—a democratic republic with direct election by citizens of other citizens to represent us, We the People. "Democracy" accurately describes, however, the direct ability and power of citizens through education, advocacy and organizing to influence other citizens, the media and elected officials through organizations, campaigns and social movements.
>
> "Democracy" is also an accurate description of the several ways We the People in many states directly govern and bypass elected representatives. These include the initiative, referendum and recall–the power of citizens to create laws, reverse laws and remove elected representatives.
>
> Whether democracy, republic, or democratic republic, they (and we) are all effectively weakened when corporations possess inalienable constitutional rights to influence public opinion, shape public laws, mold public officials and intimidate public communities.
>
> Non-profits do serve a different function than for-profit corporations, as do unions. But these powers and privileges need to be spelled out legislatively—through a democratic process—not granted by the legal system under the Constitution.[5]

Elsewhere, the same website says:

> "Our world is in terrible crisis. Solutions to the problems we face are not being implemented because 'We the People' do not have control over our own government."[6]

Here is the constitutional amendment proposed by movetoamend.org:

> Section 1. [Artificial Entities Such as Corporations Do Not Have Constitutional Rights]
>
> The rights protected by the Constitution of the United States are the rights of natural persons only.
>
> Artificial entities established by the laws of any State, the United States, or any foreign state shall have no rights under this Constitution and are subject to regulation by the People, through Federal, State, or local law.
>
> The privileges of artificial entities shall be determined by the People, through Federal, State, or local law, and shall not be construed to be inherent or inalienable.

Section 2. [Money is Not Free Speech]

Federal, State, and local government shall regulate, limit, or prohibit contributions and expenditures, including a candidate's own contributions and expenditures, to ensure that all citizens, regardless of their economic status, have access to the political process, and that no person gains, as a result of their money, substantially more access or ability to influence in any way the election of any candidate for public office or any ballot measure.

Federal, State, and local government shall require that any permissible contributions and expenditures be publicly disclosed.

The judiciary shall not construe the spending of money to influence elections to be speech under the First Amendment.[7]

Libertytreefoundation.org adds this bit of wisdom:

> Democratic Federalism:
> This country, with its institutions, belongs to the people who inhabit it. Whenever they shall grow weary of the existing government, they can exercise their constitutional right of amending it, or exercise their revolutionary right to overthrow it.
> —Abraham Lincoln
>
> Whenever any Form of Government becomes destructive of these ends, it is the Right of the People to alter or to abolish it, and to institute new Government, laying its foundation on such principles and organizing its powers in such form, as to them shall seem most likely to effect their Safety and Happiness.
> —U.S. Declaration of Independence

Finally, Movetoamend.org adds this encouraging insight:

> Americans have woken to a new political reality, a realignment in the U.S. such that today, federal power is championed by oligarchs, and local power by democrats. This realignment represents a return to pre-Cold War political realities, in which capital owned federal power, and the labor-farm coalition championed the 10th Amendment, municipal home rule, the cooperative commonwealth, and local democracy.[8]

Another significant progressive effort can be found on the Internet at www.wolf-pac.com. Focused on the Citizens United Case, this effort is typical of many left-leaning grassroots campaigns; the website does not disclose who set it up or who launched the effort. Also, typically, it is supported by younger people, who are active and enthused.

Wolf-Pac is committed to achieving an Article V convention. On May 2, a resolution seeking the convention was adopted by the legislature of the State of Vermont, a clear, though unheralded, victory for Wolf-Pac.

HARMONY AT HARVARD

Republicans and Democrats? Liberals and conservatives? The Left and the Right? Fox News and MSNBC, for Heaven's sake? Together? At the same place? In the same room?

It really happened. I was there at the Harvard University Law School along with more than 400 other folks who came from near and far to talk about the United States of America. About what's wrong with our country. And about what can be done to fix it.

Billed as "ConConCon," it was a conference designed to launch a campaign for calling a convention under Article V of the U.S. Constitution to consider amendments.[9]

It would be a convention that could give the people of the states a way to change the way politics works in Washington, DC. It would be a convention that could talk about things and propose things that Congress will never talk about and never do.

Term limits. Balanced budgets. And the money. Money that flows like raw sewage from K Street to the Capital. Money that corrupts. Money that influences. Money that changes our nation from a democratic republic to a sinister oligarchy of career politicians, corporate fat cats, ward healing bosses, and the lobbyists who tie them all together.

I went like Marley's ghost. Ten or fifteen years older than anyone in the room, I was writing and speaking about a convention when many of them were watching Sesame Street. It warmed my heart to see and hear this new generation of patriots.

Larry Lessig, the brilliant, liberal, Harvard professor, leading an all star cadre of academics and activists, keynoting the conference from the left with a witty and passionate power point presentation. Mark Meckler, the self-effacing small town lawyer from northern California, whose Lincolnesque eloquence has thrust him into the leadership of the Tea Party Patriots, making the case for his constituents' support of an Article V convention.

If the room was packed with citizens who came to listen and learn, to find out what can be done about the mess in Washington and see how they can lend a hand, it was also sprinkled with drum beaters who brought their own agendas, and touted their particular versions of the road to revival.

They all have high sounding names, websites, plans and ideas. The Alliance for Democracy. Americans United to Rebuild Democracy. Public Check on Congress. The Madison Amendment. Move To Amend. WeThe-People. Rootstrikers.

A cacophony of solutions for the same laundry list of problems, looking for harmony. Trying to find the common ground. What can we do together? Where do we go from here? Annabel Park, a co-founder of the Coffee Party said it was like being on a first date. So far, so good. Now, what's next?

It was, indeed, a most remarkable coming together. The speeches were uniformly marked with civility and deference. While several, including the distinguished Harvard University Professor, Lawrence Tribe, were skeptical about the wisdom or efficacy of a convention, there was no debunking, no ridicule, no attempt to stifle the common effort.

Only one voice sang off key; a fanatic, radical socialist who used his minute at the microphone to hawk his Socialist Constitution and accuse the Tea Party of racism. He got an audible groan from the crowd and an admonition from the chair.

I went to Cambridge with some flyers of my own, inviting conferees to register as delegates to Convention USA, a place on the Internet where ordinary people can work together to find the best solutions to our national dilemma.

One speaker at the conference presented a particularly interesting point of view. His name is Richard Parker. A Harvard law professor for more than thirty-five years, Parker describes himself as a populist, and insists that the true dichotomy in American politics is not between the left and the right, but between the elite and the folks.

True to that definition, Parker wrote a book entitled *Here the People Rule*,[10] and he lends his support as General Chairman to the Citizens Flag Alliance, a grassroots organization supporting a constitutional amendment to authorize Congress to outlaw desecration of the American flag. Professor Parker may be an anomaly at Harvard, but a flag amendment would generate support from the vast majority of Americans.

I must confess that I left Harvard with the crescent conviction that there are vast numbers of what Professor Parker calls "the folks" who would answer the call for an Article V convention.

If Harvard was a first date, maybe those good folks will want to go steady some day. The vehicle is right there at www.conventionusa.org.

CONSENSUS

Let's face it, an Article V convention, although it is limited to proposing amendments to the 1787 Constitution, is nonetheless a constitutional convention. It deals with the United States Constitution. Its proposals will need the ratification of three-quarters of the states, and that goal certainly requires a broad consensus of the American people.

To be successful, constitutional amendments must appear to be the work of truly impartial authors. Public perception of the impartiality of the convention will largely depend on who gavels the convention to order. Short of Pope Francis and the Dalai Lama, there is practically no one on the planet who would be perceived as neutral in political affairs.

Convention USA, a nonprofit corporation which operates a website at www.conventionusa.org, has been in existence for several years. When delegates from two thirds of the states were registered, the convention was called to order. Several meetings were held on the Internet. Delegates adopted rules and on September 23, 2012, with the votes of a majority of the delegates and a majority of the States represented, I was elected Permanent Chairman of Convention USA.

My election was neither much of an honor nor much of a surprise. I am, after all, the founder of Convention USA and its principal financier. Much as I am proud of how far we have come and excited about the vision of a live convention, I have no illusions that I am either competent or qualified to gavel the convention to order in Saint Louis.

But I think I know who should be on the podium on that day. The United States of America is extremely fortunate, at this time in its history, to have two former Presidents who are both young enough and vigorous enough to chair a constitutional convention.

It is equally serendipitous that former Presidents Bush and Clinton are identified with the two major political parties; that they were both Governors of their states, and therefore have an appreciation of American federalism; that they have both gained in stature since retiring from the Oval Office, and both enjoy the admiration, respect, and gratitude of the nation; and of singular good fortune, they have developed a comradeship in charitable and civic endeavors which evidences their disposition and capacity to cooperate for the common good.

The positive results that would flow from these appointments are almost too numerous to catalog. In addition to instant recognition and prestige for the convention, with all the attendant financial support, civic approbation, and media attention that would cascade from the announcement, there is the further substantive assumption that, operating under the gavel of two former Commanders in Chief, the convention would not be likely to "run away."

Despite hailing from different political parties, both Mr. Bush and Mr. Clinton reside philosophically in the main currents of political thought. Neither of them would inspire radical or dissident activities on the floor.

Here's a quote from Bill Clinton that could be a keynote for the convention:

> In other words, our constitution was designed by people who were idealistic but not ideological. There's a big difference. You can have a philosophy that tends to be liberal or conservative but still be open to evidence, experience, and argument. That enables people with honest differences to find practical, principled compromise.[11]

And another from George Bush:

> We'll have our disagreements. Civility does not require us to abandon deeply-held beliefs. Civility does not demand casual creeds and colorless convictions. Americans have always believed that civility and firm resolve could live easily with one another. But civility does mean that our public debate ought to be free from bitterness and anger, rancor and ill-will. We have an obligation to make our case, not to demonize our opponents. As the Book of James reminds us, fresh water and salt water cannot flow from the same spring.[12]

Those are the guidelines that must instruct a constitutional convention if it is to propose amendments that can command a consensus of the American people.

Our former presidents are a national treasure. Both of them already receive adequate compensation, support, and security from the federal government; they are, in a very real sense, the most visible, powerful, and available First Responders to our national emergency.

Their commission would not be overwhelming. Roberts Rules of Order permit the presiding officer of a convention to pass the gavel to a chairman pro tem; there would be no need for the Presidents to devote long days and nights to the tedium of convention business. Their formal and actual authority to make the critical decisions reserved to the Permanent Chair of the convention is what would make their participation genuine and significant.

I have no illusions that either Mr. Bush or Mr. Clinton would rejoice at or relish receiving this invitation. Neither would likely agree without the concurrence of the other, nor would either embrace the convention in the face of widespread opposition or apathy.

Still, no one who loves America and grieves over her dismay will not share the hope that they would agree to make this last historic sacrifice for the nation and the people they have so honorably served.

NOTES

1. http://conventionofstates.com/the-strategy/.
2. http://conventionofstates.com/wp-content/uploads/2014/03/Application-for-a-Convention-of-States-v.5.pdf.
3. http://www.wethepeoplefoundation.org/UPDATE/Update2011-10-29.htm.
4. https://movetoamend.org/frequently-asked-questions.
5. Ibid.
6. Ibid.
7. https://movetoamend.org/wethepeopleamendment.
8. http://democracysquare.org/areas-focus/liberty-tree-foundation/democratic-federalism.
9. http://www.conconcon.org/.
10. Richard Parker, *Here the People Rule: A Constitutional Populist Manifesto* (Cambridge, MA: Harvard University Press, 1998).
11. William J. Clinton, *Back to Work: Why We Need Smart Government for a Strong Economy* (New York: Knopf, 2011).
12. George W. Bush, Remarks at the President's National Prayer Breakfast, February 1, 2001.

II

The Agenda

Chapter Five

Legislative Reform

In December of 1955 there was a special election in the Thirteenth Congressional District of Michigan to select a successor to the incumbent Congressman John Dingell. I was the Republican nominee. My Democratic opponent was John Dingell, Jr. the son of the deceased Congressman.

There was a newspaper strike at the time, and the voter turnout was extremely light. John was elected by a vote of around 19,000 to 6,000. He has been in the United States Congress ever since, and is now the longest serving member of Congress in the history of the nation.

In 1955, the Thirteenth Congressional District consisted of the Sixteenth Ward of the city of Detroit, a narrow rectangle less than two miles wide stretching North from the Detroit River about eight miles to the City limits.

Over the years the district has been redefined many times. Today, Congressman Dingell represents the Twelfth District of Michigan, a thirty-eight-sided monstrosity that meanders nearly forty miles from the shore of Lake Erie near the mouth of the Detroit River to a point somewhere west of Ann Arbor in Washtenaw County.

Presumably, Dingell maintains a qualifying residence in Michigan, but his actual home is in the nation's capital or environs. That's where he lives and works.

Representative Dingell's preeminence as the nation's senior legislator also makes him the poster boy for what is wrong with the government of our nation. Without meaning to suggest anything personally derogatory about John Dingell, who has been a friend of mine ever since we were opponents more than half a century ago, it is true that, as a general proposition, Members of Congress are career politicians who are elected and reelected every two years, who must raise massive amounts of money to finance their campaigns, and who are habitually drawn into the vortex of lobby influenced special interest legislation.

Much has been written and said about the United States Congress in the last few years. The website realclearpolitics.com accumulates various polling data and publishes a synthesis. The Real Clear Politics Congressional average approval rating of seven major polls for the period January 12, 2014 through February 17, 2014 showed that 12.3 percent of Americans approve of the work being done by Congress and 84.3 percent disapprove.

No doubt the snafu over the rollout of ObamaCare has exacerbated the disgust of many voters who were already upset over the fact that the massive 2,000-page law was not read by Members of Congress who voted for it. But such widely publicized fiascos are only the obvious and notorious Congressional failings. The every day operations of the Congress provide a more enduring and bedrock cause of voter disenchantment.

Take, for example, the relationship between members of Congress and the lobbyists who swarm around the Capital. Harvard professor Lawrence Lessig, in his powerful treatise, *Republic, Lost*, details what he calls the "gift economy" in Washington.

Federal law prohibits bribing members of Congress. Giving, receiving, offering, or soliciting anything of value for the purpose of influencing or affecting the vote of a Congressman or Senator is a crime, as is doing so to influence any official act of any federal official.

But bribery involves a quid pro quo. Buying votes in Congress is a crime. Giving money to a Congressional campaign fund is not. Lessig describes an environment inside the beltway in which lobbyists work at becoming friends and supporters of members of Congress. Typically, they target Congressmen and Senators who have already indicated convictions that favor their clients' interests.

These friendly officeholders are targeted. Fundraising events are organized. All manner of favors, large and small, are proffered with nothing asked in return. Senators must run for reelection in statewide campaigns. Even in the smallest states this requires a lot of money. Mike Enzi, Senator from the nation's smallest state, Wyoming, which has only a little over half a million inhabitants spent $3.4 million to be reelected in 2008.

A senatorial campaign in California has a price tag in excess of $100 million. It should come as no surprise then, to hear that Senators typically spend a substantial part of each six-year term banking funds for the next election. As a matter of fact, the practice is so common that a phrase has been invented to describe the period of time devoted to campaigning. It is call the "election cycle."

And a cycle it surely is. Round and round it goes from one election to the next with no respite in between. No sooner does a Senator or Congressperson take the oath of office than the solicitation of funds for the next election begins.

Senators, of course, run statewide. Their constituencies vary from 563,000 in Wyoming to 38 million in California. Members of the House of Representatives are elected from districts. Still, their constituencies vary from Wyoming's 563,000 to over a million in neighboring Montana. The average is about 750,000.

It is apparent therefore, that much of the mendacity so commonplace in the nation's capital is the product of elections in large constituencies. In turn, large constituencies and expensive elections are the natural breeding grounds for professional, career politicians.

People don't like professional, career politicians. Still, professional, career politicians, by definition, are men and women who are able to win elections. Thus, the paradox: an unpopular Congress full of popular incumbents who get reelected time after time.

Sort of reminds you of the old Yogi Bera punch line about the restaurant:"It's too crowded. Nobody goes there anymore."

So what can be done about it? How do we sever the symbiosis between big money lobbyists and influence peddlers and the representatives of the people? How do we achieve the objective of making the Congress responsive to the people?

TERM LIMITS

One reform that has a great deal of support is to impose term limits on members of Congress. A website called TermLimits.org claims that support for limiting the terms of elected officials is the largest grassroots movement in the nation.

In the last decades of the twentieth century, a number of states passed laws setting term limits on their representatives in Congress. These state restrictions were tested in court and eventually wound up before the United States Supreme Court. Its decision *U.S. Term Limits, Inc. v. Thornton*, 514 U.S. 779 (1995), settled the matter adversely to the petitioners.[1]

The Court's decision was based on the simple fact that members of Congress are constitutional officers of the United States and their qualifications for office are enumerated in the U.S. Constitution. Those qualifications do not include term limits. Ergo, there can be none. It is settled, then, that if there are to be term limits for members of Congress, they must be specified in the United States Constitution.

Among the supporters of term limits is the best selling author and feisty radio talk show host, Mark Levin. In his immensely popular book, *The Liber-*

ty Amendments, Levin offers the following proposed constitutional amendment:

> SECTION 1: No person may serve more than twelve years as a member of Congress, whether such service is exclusively in the House or the Senate or combined in both Houses.
> SECTION 2: Upon ratification of this Article, an incumbent member of Congress whose term exceeds the twelve-year limit shall complete the current term, but thereafter will be ineligible for further service as a member of Congress.[2]

Perhaps no other person in America is as entitled to claim the title "Father of Term Limits" than is Mr. George E. Will, the famed newspaper columnist and Pulitzer Prize winning author. In *Restoration: Congress, Term Limits and the Recovery of Deliberative Democracy*, Will argues cogently for the imposition of limits on Congressional service.

Beginning on page 3, he has this to say:

> Americans today favor term limits by substantial margins. In every region and every demographic group, there is a substantial majority for term limits. This majority may have, as yet, only a shallow commitment to a reform that is only superficially understood. However, the more deeply Americans understand the philosophical justifications for term limits, and the probable consequences of limits, the more intense the support for limits should become. One lesson of American history is that when a majority of Americans have a strong and protracted desire for something, they get it. This book is an attempt to nourish the intensity and staying power of the desire for term limits. My aim is to help transform this desire from a lightly held preference into a deeply felt, because fully comprehended, conviction.[3]

Among the interesting charts Will provides is one showing that the number of Senators with twelve or more years of service has gradually increased over the last century until, in recent years it has reached almost half of that august body. Other charts demonstrate that about 80 percent of Congressional incumbents in both Houses are typically reelected.[4]

Will elaborates on the grievous damage to the Republic that has been done in the frantic chase to protect incumbents' reelection. One battlefield on which partisan electoral combat is most vicious is the area of reapportionment. The U.S. Supreme Court ruling in the case of *Baker v. Carr*, 369 U.S. 186 (1962) established the rule of "one man one vote." That decision ushered in a new and exacerbated era of gerrymandering that would have delighted the man whose name was given to the practice of creating favorable election districts.

Elbridge Gerry was the Governor of Massachusetts, who, in 1812 signed into law a bill that created a representative district, the map of which resembled a salamander. The word "gerrymander" was coined by the *Boston Globe* as the caption of a cartoon showing the grotesquely shaped election district created by the Jeffersonians to defeat the Federalists.[5]

Gerrymandering was elevated to an exact science when the sloganized "one man one vote" decision in *Baker v. Carr* became wedded to the sophistication of modern computer technology.

Using the small units of measurement known as census tracts, and ignoring all boundaries of local units of government, it is possible to design districts that achieve preposterous mathematical equality. They are preposterous because they are attempting to locate human beings and human beings are not stationary. The State of New York, for example, after the 2000 census, created districts for its twenty-nine members of the national House of Representatives of 654,360 persons. Plus or minus 1 person! Thus the smallest district had 654,359 residents and the largest had 654,361 residents.

Considering the fact that it takes some months for the Census Bureau to complete its work and publish results, it is a practical impossibility to know the exact population even of a small, 4,000 person census tract, much less identify the location of 654,360 ambulatory human beings.

But the ingenuity and self-interest of man being what they are, the game of reapportionment is played with consummate skill by entrenched politicians. George Will includes maps of four of the most egregious specimens on pages 43–46 of his book. They resemble nothing quite so much as Rorschach Tests designed by a deranged psychiatrist.

Will gives us a peek at a principal reason for all of this by quoting the 1982 amendment to the Voting Rights Act of 1965:

> 42 USC 1973b A violation of subsection (a) is established if, based on the totality of circumstances, it is shown that the political processes leading to nomination or election in the State or political subdivision are not open to participation by members of a class of citizens protected by subsection (a) in that its members have less opportunity than other members of the electorate to participate in the political process and to elect representatives of their choice. THE EXTENT TO WHICH MEMBERS OF A PROTECTED CLASS HAVE BEEN ELECTED TO OFFICE IN THE STATE OR POLITICAL SUBDIVISION IS ONE CIRCUMSTANCE WHICH MAY BE CONSIDERED: Provided, that nothing in this section establishes a right to have members of protected class elected in numbers equal to their proportion in the population.[6]

The Census Bureau doesn't just count people. It asks a lot of personal questions. It tracks race, sex, ethnicity, wealth, occupation: everything except flat out asking what political party you vote for. It's all information which computer-assisted political junkies can message into predictable voting districts that will protect incumbent officeholders.

George Will believes that, even if the horrors of gerrymandering cannot be ended, their effects can be ameliorated by the adoption of Term Limits. But the connection between gerrymandering and extended tenure in office is not a relationship of cause and effect. Tailoring districts to favor a black or Hispanic candidate isn't going to change just because the incumbent is ineligible to run for reelection.

A Congressman limited to twelve years in office will run for reelection five times. She will win the first term as a newcomer, but after that it will be same old, same old, until the twelve years are up. She will be courted by the minions of K Street. She will contract the same disease of incumbency that George Will and Mark Levin rail against. Term limits will only insure that every twelve years the cycle will be repeated.

This is no reason to throw up our hands in frustration and be resigned to the rule of hated career politicians. No indeed, term limits have something to offer. But career politicians are not the problem per se. The problem is that the national House of Representatives, which was created by the constitution to represent the people of the United States, does not adequately or properly represent the people of the United States.

Article I of the Constitution says that representation in the House must be proportional to the population. It is not. The Founders of our nation, and the constitution they ratified contemplated that the size of the House of Representatives would be adjusted at every decennial census in order to retain a proper ratio of representatives to constituents. This has not been done in more than one hundred years.

Too many career politicians who get reelected too many times, raise and spend too much money on their campaigns, and cavort too cozily with the big money people whose agents swarm around the Capital Building is not a problem that will go away with the adoption of Term Limits. You can't cure lung cancer by sucking on cough drops.

Of course, there's nothing wrong with cough drops. If they help sooth the cough, that's fine. But they won't cure the cancer. And if taking cough drops becomes a substitute for chemotherapy, it will help to kill you.

HOW BIG A HOUSE?

The man's name is Jeff Quidam, or so he says. I believe it is a pseudonym. Quidam is Latin for "someone." I believe his real name is Jeff Strode and that he is the CEO of Thirty-Thousand.org, which operates a website at www.thirty-thousand.org.

I don't know much about him, except that he is a family man, skilled in computer technology, a patriot, and a student of constitutional history. My kind of guy.

The website, www.thirty-thousand.org, is a cornucopia of information about the U.S. Constitution, particularly Article I that establishes the national legislature. On that website, you can find an excellent pamphlet entitled *Taking Back Our Republic*, and you can print it out at no charge. I did that, and I recommend it: www.thirty-thousand.org/documents/TTO_Pamphlet.pdf

The pamphlet bears a copyright mark and shows the owner as Thirty-Thousand.org. The pamphlet tells us that:

> Thirty-Thousand.org is a non-partisan and non-profit organization which conducts research on, and educates the public about, the insidious degradation of representative democracy in the United States resulting from Congress's long-standing practice of constricting the number of Representatives (in the federal House) relative to the total population.

Given that purpose, I presume that my extensive quotes from the pamphlet will be regarded as fair commentary calculated to educate the public as intended by thirty-thousand.org. Let's begin at the beginning. Article I, Section 1 of the federal Constitution says, "All legislative power herein granted shall be vested in a Congress which shall consist of a Senate and House of Representatives."

Section 2 provides that Representatives shall be apportioned among the States "according to their respective numbers." It then goes on to say that there will be an actual enumeration within three years and every ten years thereafter. Section 2 then provides that "the number of Representatives shall not exceed one for every thirty thousand, but every State shall have at least one Representative."

Those numbers were not universally agreeable. Melancton Smith, a delegate to the New York ratifying convention could foresee problems. In his view the "respectable yeomanry" of the nation would be excluded from so small a group of lawmakers. He feared "corruption and combination" and opined:

> A great politician has said that every man has his price. I hope this is not true in all its extent; but I ask the gentleman (Alexander Hamilton) to inform me what government there is in which it has not been practiced.[7]

Smith went on to show that with a bare quorum in both houses; fourteen in the Senate and thirty-three in the House, a majority of a quorum would consist of seven in the Senate and seventeen in the House, and he asked:

> Can the liberties of three millions of people be securely trusted in the hands of twenty-four men? Is it prudent to commit to so small a number the decision of the great questions which will come before them? Reason revolts at the idea.[8]

A minority at the Pennsylvania Ratifying Convention was of like mind. On December 18, 1787 a group led by Robert Whitehall published the "Dissent of the Minority of the Convention" in Pennsylvania newspapers. They challenged the ratio of 30,000 to one and were suspicious that the number of Representatives would be increased over time as the population would grow. Their report concluded that:

> The liberties, happiness, interests, and great concerns of the whole United States may be dependent upon the integrity, virtue, wisdom and knowledge of 25 or 26 men. How inadequate and unsafe a representation! Inadequate because the sense and views of 3 or 4 millions of people diffused over so extensive a territory comprising such various climates, products, habits, interests and opinions cannot be collected in so small a body.[9]

They added some words that should give pause to the Americans of 2014:

> "The number of representatives will probably be continued at 65, although the population may swell to treble what it now is; unless revolution should effect a change."[10]

In Massachusetts, Doctor John Taylor argued that the size of the House of Representatives was too small, and he pointed to the legislature of the Bay State, which alone had 150 legislators.[11]

Supporters of ratification began to take their cue from James Madison who addressed the issue in the Federalist Papers. Conceding that the national legislature was small when compared to the State legislatures, Madison argued that the size of the legislature was sufficient in light of the limited jurisdiction of the national government under the constitution.

James Wilson of Pennsylvania argued that the national government was to be one of limited, enumerated powers, and that a small legislative body was sufficient to handle the general business of the United States. The idea of a central government dealing with the minutia of civic concerns at the local level for the entire nation would be unthinkable. He opined:

> "To support, with vigor, a single government over the whole extent of the United States, would demand a system of the most unqualified and the most unremitted despotism."[12]

ARTICLE THE FIRST

Few Americans realize that the original Bill of Rights consisted of not ten, but twelve, proposed amendments. The ten amendments actually ratified and made part of our Constitution as the Bill of Rights, were in fact the last ten of the twelve proposed.

The second amendment proposed in 1788 provided that members of Congress could not raise their own salaries effective immediately, but would have to wait until they had been reelected before receiving an increased compensation. That amendment failed ratification among the original thirteen states, and sat in the bowels of Congress for two hundred years until a student at the University of Texas named Gregory Watson discovered it and brought it to the attention of modern legislators. It is now the Twenty-Seventh Amendment, having been ratified in 1992.

The first of the twelve amendments proposed in 1788, referred to as Article the First, was intended to answer the question "How big is the House of Representatives?" It was never ratified.

It provided that there should be one representative for every 30,000 people until the size of the House reached 100, then, there would be one representative for every 40,000 until there were two hundred in the House. That threshold would be reached when the census showed a population of 8,000,000.

As the amendment was considered and passed by the House of Representatives, it provided that when the House reached 200 members, it would thereafter have a minimum of one representative for every 50,000 inhabitants in a state.

Unfortunately, the Senate disagreed and amended the House bill to provide that when the House reached 200 members, the ratio would thereafter be one representative for every 60,000 inhabitants. This difference required that the two versions of the proposed amendment be referred to a conference committee to resolve the problem.

Unhappily, or perhaps tragically, the report of the conference committee showed neither the House version nor the Senate version. What came out of committee, and because of an urgent need to deliver the twelve proposed amendments to the waiting state legislatures, what was officially proposed by Congress and sent to the thirteen states was a garbled version of the House bill.

Instead of providing that, when the membership of the House reached 200 it would thereafter consist of not *less* than one representative for every 50,000 people, it said that the House would consist of not *more* than one representative for every fifty thousand residents.

What was intended to be a minimum became a maximum. So the proposed amendment now contained a strange contradiction. When the population would reach 8 million, the minimum size of the House of Representatives would be 200, but the maximum would be 160.

Several states ratified Article the First, even with its confused language, but shortly, the error being discovered, state legislatures simply ignored the proposed amendment.

History is replete with curious, inexplicable events. In the case of Article the First, the scrivener's error in substituting the word "more" for the word "less" has lead the United States of America to a place in its history which should never have been.

Because Article the first was not ratified, the matter of determining the size of the House of Representatives was left to the discretion of the members of Congress themselves. Unlike the courts, where decisions are supposed to be made based on logic, reason and precedent, a legislative body is said to 'work its will.' That is to say a legislature does what its members want to do.

The constitution of 1787 spelled out the number of representatives each of the thirteen states would have. After the census of 1790 Congress determined that there should be 105 seats in the House, one for every 33,000 people in a state.

The ratio of one to 33,000 was used again in 1800, resulting in 142 seats. In 1810 the ratio was increased to one for every 35,000, and the House grew to 181 members.

In 1820, they used a ratio of one to 40,000. The House then had 213 seats, which increased to 240 in 1830 when the ratio was one to every 47,700 inhabitants. In 1840, however, the number of seats was decreased to 233 and the ratio increased to 70,680 people for each representative.

In 1842 Congress enacted a law that required the states to create individual Congressional districts. Until that time some states were electing multiple Congressmen from the larger cities and counties. From this point on, Congress no longer established ratios of people to representatives when reapportioning the House. Instead, every ten years they would make the decision backwards; that is, they would first decide how large the House should be, and then apportion the seats to the states according to their population.

Using this method, Congress expanded the House to 241 in 1860; 283 in 1870; 325 in 1880; 358 in 1890; 386 in 1900, and 433 after the census of 1910. Two more seats were added in 1911 to accommodate Arizona and New Mexico, making the total 435.

Then in 1929, Congress passed an act permanently establishing the size of the House of Representatives at 435. It has remained at that number ever since, with one brief sojourn to 437 members when Hawaii and Alaska joined the Union.

The bottom line is that we have had a House of Representatives consisting of 435 persons for over 100 years, during which time the population of the United States has increased from 92,228,496 to over 308 millions.

WHY 435?

Thirty-thousand.org quotes Missouri Representative, Ralph Lozier, speaking during the debate on the 1929 Act:

> I am unalterably opposed to limiting the membership of the House to the arbitrary number of 435. Why 435? Why not 400? Why not 300? Why not 250, 450, 535, or 600? Why is this number 435 sacred? What merit is there in having a membership of 435 that we would not have if the membership were 335 or 535? There is no sanctity in the number 435. There is absolutely no reason, philosophy, or common sense in arbitrarily fixing the membership of the House at 435 or at any other number. [13]

Again, the thirty-thousand.org pamphlet quotes from *Federalist #55*:

> It will not be thought an extravagant conjecture that the first census will, at the rate of one for every thirty thousand, raise the number of representatives to at least one hundred. . . . At the expiration of twenty-five years, according to the computed rate of increase, the number of representatives will amount to two hundred, and of fifty years, to four hundred.

The pamphlet details the factors that contribute to higher reelection rates among representatives with larger districts. The ability to solicit funds generally and to secure nonfinancial help from various advocacy groups, opportunities for free media coverage and attention, and the franking privilege that allows substantial free mailings to constituents all favor incumbents over challengers.

We are reminded that money is the mother's milk of politics and that in 2008, the average war chest of incumbent Congressmen was $1.4 million. Raising that kind of money isn't easy. It takes a lot of hard work and attention. Especially, it takes time; time away from other activities, like reading bills that have been introduced or are being voted upon.

Certainly, if incumbents have to work at raising campaign funds, how much more money must a challenger have to bank in order to mount credible opposition to a sitting Congressman?

On page 9 of the pamphlet, the author presents a startling chart which traces the relationship between the number of constituents represented by a member of Congress and the number of years of service. The correlation is almost perfect. The bigger the district, the longer the Representative stays in office.

The first reaction of most people, when told that the size of the House of Representatives, if the recommendations of our founders were to be followed, would swell to something like 6,000 members, is to laugh or to say something like, "We certainly don't want MORE of those awful people!"

The image of jamming thousands of representatives into the Capitol, with all the attendant ruckus and disorder induces an instant negative perception. It takes a little patience to get past that initial vision.

Still, given a few moments to think about it, to tally up the pluses and minuses, and to get outside the jailhouse of the status quo, most reasonable folks will begin to see that it is not such a bad idea at all. Why, for example, should the size of our national legislature be frozen in tradition? Why should it depend on the size of the room or the size of the building? Or even be controlled by the number of seats or desks we happen to have?

In 1787, they didn't even have bullhorns. There were no sound systems, no electronic communication of any kind. A Congress had to fit in a single room if they were all to hear what was being said. Today, there are college classes being conducted remotely. The professor is in a room hundreds of miles from the students, and students are gathered in dozens of rooms miles away from the instructor and miles away from each other. They can all hear the professor. They can all see the blackboard. They can all ask questions, and if called upon, they can all recite.

It took weeks to get from North Carolina to Philadelphia in 1787. Today the podium is as close as the screen on your computer. Members of Congress in 2014 are a big deal. They represent hundreds of thousands of citizens—750,000 on average. They make a salary of $174,000 per year and they get an average of $1.3 million annually for membership expenses, for an average staff of eighteen people, for travel and communication.

Under the Constitution as it now reads, members of Congress do not have to live in their districts. They need only be inhabitants of their state. As a practical matter, because of continued reelection, most Congressmen, like Representative Dingell, actually live in the Capital City. And, of course, that's where they work. Downtown Washington, DC. That's where their offices are, that's where they can be found almost every day. That's where they park their car, eat lunch, and mingle.

Thirty-thousand.org tells us that in 2008 there were nearly 15,000 registered lobbyists in the United States, about twenty-eight for every Congressman and Senator. That year, he says, they reported spending over $3.2 billion, equivalent to $6 million per member of Congress.

Now if we ask that chap who giggled at the idea of having 6,000 Congressmen how he would feel about Congressmen who 1) make less salary, 2) get less expense money, and 3) live and work in their districts, perhaps the reaction is not nearly so flippant.

It should take no citation of authority to assert that smaller districts would bring representatives closer to their constituents; that they would enable poorly financed, working-class candidates to campaign door to door, that more citizens will see and meet their representatives in person; that television advertising and professionally engineered public relations will have much less sway on the voters, much less impact on elections.

More members of Congress will be citizen-representatives, living in their districts among the people they speak for. They will be able to stand up for what they and their neighbors think and believe. Campaigns will be based on principles rather than carefully vetted 'positions' on controversial issues.

An especially important benefit associated with increasing the size of the House is the extent to which it will reduce the influence of political parties on our government. Here I must credit Mr. Strode for some very wise and perceptive comments. Beginning on page 12, the Thiry-thousand.org pamphlet says:

> George Washington's 1796 "Farewell Address" included an extensive warning about the "baneful effects" of political parties in which he observed that: "They [the parties] serve to organize faction, to give it an artificial and extraordinary force—to put in place of the delegated will of the Nation, the will of a party [who are] often a small but artful and enterprising minority of the Community."[14]

There can be no doubt that party affiliation is the major factor in elections in our present oversized congressional districts. Political parties are the brand names of politicians. When the television commentators summarize election returns, the principal story line has to do with the number of seats won or lost by the two major political parties.

No doubt party affiliations would continue to exist in an expanded House, but much of the discipline would be lost. With representatives living and working in their home states, the aura of each party will be affected by the location of the district. Mississippi Republicans differ from New York Republicans. And California Democrats don't share a lot with North Carolina Democrats.

Lyndon Johnson was famous for his ability, both as a Senator and as President, to buttonhole legislators and physically intimidate them to garner votes. That sort of politicking won't prosper when members don't share the same cloakroom. The herd instinct will be softened by distance.

Of course, the logic of a two party system is not likely to disappear. Every human decision is essentially a binary function. Yes or no. Either do or don't. But where candidates are able to interact more directly with their constituents voting patterns are more likely to be influenced by the people in the district than the party leadership in Washington.

With a larger House of Representatives, the influence of anonymous professional staff will be reduced. Representatives will be forced to read what they are expected to vote on. Which brings me to another subject.

SINGLE SUBJECT LEGISLATION

Article IV, Section 24 of the 1963 Constitution of Michigan provides:

> No law shall embrace more than one object, which shall be expressed in its title. No bill shall be altered or amended on its passage through either house so as to change its original purpose as determined by its total content and not alone by its title.

The obvious reason for this constitutional provision is to prevent the consideration of so-called "omnibus" bills, voluminous, multi-purpose legislation in which a multitude of unrelated provisions address different problems, amend numerous sections of various codes, and deal with a variety of legislative purposes.

The practice of adopting omnibus bills provides opportunities for individual representatives to include special purpose provisions that benefit their districts. When enough members have ownership of some small piece of an omnibus bill, its chances of adoption improve.

In a milieu of omnibus bills it is quite possible, perhaps very common, that without targeted special benefits included for various members, the entire bill would fail passage. It can hardly be said that the people's business is being attended to when a bill that nobody wants is adopted because a majority have been thrown a bone in the fine print.

Omnibus legislation has another unhappy dimension: It is so long and complicated that Representatives do not read the bills. It's not just the time. Bills that are drafted by professional staff, both in Congressional offices and in the offices of the multitude of executive agencies are typically complicated, convoluted concoctions.

Self-interest plays a large role in the complicating of government. People who make a living drafting and explaining complicated laws have no motive to join the "Plain English" revolution which is beginning to take hold in our law schools.

Our constitutional forefathers wanted the Congress to be populated in part by persons they described as "yeomen" by which they intended to describe what we would call the working class. It is not difficult to understand how intimidated Joe the Plumber would be surrounded by a coterie of sesquipedalians.

Thomas Aquinas defined law as a rule of reason, ordained and promulgated by proper authority for the common good. Philosophically and practically law must be promulgated. The Code of Hammurabi was posted on the pillars of Babylon for all to see. Moses presented God's commandments on tablets of stone where the people could read them.

Here is a taste of what our national government proffers as promulgation of law:

> **Tax Table or Tax Computation Worksheet.** If your taxable income is less than $100,000, you must use the Tax Table, later in these instructions, to figure your tax. Be sure you use the correct column. If your taxable income is $100,000 or more, use the Tax Computation Worksheet right after the Tax Table.
>
> However, do not use the Tax Table or Tax Computation Worksheet to figure your tax if any of the following applies.
>
> **Form 8615.** Form 8615 generally must be used to figure the tax for any child who had more than $2,000 of unearned income, such as taxable interest, ordinary dividends, or capital gains (including capital gain distributions), and who either:
>
> 1. Was under age 18 at the end of 2013,
>
> 2. Was age18 at the end of 2013 and did not have earned income that was more than half of the child's support, or
>
> 3. Was a full-time student over age 18 and under age 24 at the end of 2013 and did not have earned income that was more than half of the child's support.
>
> But if the child files a joint return for 2013 or if neither of the child's parents was alive at the end of 2013, do not use Form 8615 to figure the child's tax.
>
> A child born on January 1, 1996, is considered to be age 18 at the end of 2013; a child born on January 1, 1995, is considered to be age 19 at the end of 2013; a child born on January 1, 1990, is considered to be age 24 at the end of 2013.
>
> **Schedule D Tax Worksheet.** If you have to file Schedule D, and line 18 or 19 of Schedule D is more than zero, use the Schedule D Tax Worksheet in the Instructions for Schedule D to figure the amount to enter on Form 1040, line 44. But if you are filing Form 2555 or 2555-EZ, you must use the Foreign Earned Income Tax Worksheet instead.

The famed French author, Alexis de Tocqueville, opined that despotism might overtake a democracy by means of a network of small, complicated rules through which the most original minds cannot penetrate; the will of man is softened, bent. Such a power does not destroy or tyrannize but enervates and stupefies a people until they lose the faculties of thinking, feeling and acting for themselves.

Single subject legislation that Representatives and the general public can get their arms around, laws written in plain English they can read and understand, will go a long way toward restoring confidence in our government.

THE SENATE

The United States Senate is supposed to represent the states. That's why it was created. The "Grand Compromise" reached in Philadelphia in 1787 was the creation of a bicameral legislature, composed of two Houses, both of which would have to agree upon any action of the Congress.

The lower house, so-called, was to be the House of Representatives, and it was to represent the people directly. Accordingly, the size of the House was to be proportional to the size of the nation, with each state having representatives proportional to its population.

The upper house was to be known as the Senate. It represented the governments of the sovereign states of the American Union. Each state would have two Senators.

Obviously, the Grand Compromise recognized the different interests of large and small states. The delegates from the small states feared that the larger states might vote them out of existence, or at least vote themselves preferences and advantages not shared with the smaller states.

So concerned were the small state delegates to the 1787 convention, that they insisted on a provision in Article V, literally protecting them from constitutional amendment. It says that no state, without its consent, shall be deprived of its equal suffrage in the Senate.

With this great sensitivity for equal status in the Senate, it is curious that the Founders specified that each state would have two Senators. Perhaps they just didn't anticipate how ingrained and structural the two party system would become.

Whatever the reason, the assignment of two Senators to each state has effectively done what the constitution forbids: it has often denied many states their equal suffrage in the United States Senate. Whenever a vote proceeds along party lines—and most of the important decisions do—states with one Republican Senator and one Democratic Senator are effectively disenfranchised.

Here are the current numbers:

There are seventeen states with two Democratic Senators.
There are fourteen states with two Republican Senators.
There are seventeen states with one Republican Senator and one Democratic Senator.
There is one state with one Republican Senator and one Independent.
There is one state with one Democratic Senator and one Independent.

So what happens when a controversial issue reaches the floor of the Senate? If, in fact, Article V of the Constitution were to be enforced, and each state given "equal suffrage" in the Senate, nothing would happen.

Even if the two Independent Senators were to vote with their state colleague, there would still be seventeen States without a voice on the issue.

How do the people in Arkansas, Arizona, Florida, Illinois, Indiana, Louisiana, Wisconsin, Missouri, Nevada, New Hampshire, New Jersey, North

Carolina, North Dakota, Ohio, Pennsylvania, and South Dakota feel about the issue?

No one will ever know. They have no voice in the United States Senate.

I don't want to sound critical of James Madison, George Washington, and their colleagues, but wouldn't it have been wiser to give each state either one Senator or three Senators? Perhaps they vetoed providing only one Senator out of concern that, if that one Senator were delayed or incapacitated, the state would lose its vote. And maybe—just maybe—someone figured out that if each state had three votes, it would be possible for a minority of the states to assemble a majority of the Senators. That would be mathematically possible.

If each state had three Senators, there would be a total of 150 votes in the upper chamber. If twenty states unanimously vote "Aye" and sixteen states cast but one "Aye" vote, there would be a majority of seventy-six Ayes. Still, thirty of the fifty states would be opposed.

There are, of course many ways to assure that the Senate actually speaks for the states. Voting by states rather than Senators is one way. If the two Senators don't agree, the Governor of the state could be empowered to break the tie.

Repealing the Seventeenth Amendment is another strategy. If Senators are appointed by the state legislatures, they might also be recalled by the legislatures, making them more accurately delegates of the states.

I am personally aligned with those who believe the Seventeenth Amendment should be repealed. Being elected state-wide, Senators are simply at-large Congressmen. A Senator's "client" if you will, is not the government of the state, but the people. Since the adoption of the Seventeenth Amendment, no one in Washington represents the state governments. And, of course, all the evils of fundraising associated with large constituencies, discussed above, are present in state-wide senatorial elections

These are all matters to be determined in convention by the delegates. It would be enough at the outset for the convention to agree that the agenda would include reforms in the national legislature.

NOTES

1. *U.S. Term Limits, Inc. v. Thornton*, 514 U.S. 779 (1995).
2. Mark Levin, *The Liberty Amendments: Restoring the American Republic* (New York: Simon and Schuster, 2013), p. 19.
3. George F. Will, *Restoration: Congress, Term Limits and the Recovery of Deliberative Democracy* (New York, The Free Press, 1992), pp. 3–4.
4. Ibid., pp. 81-83.
5. www.randomhouse.com/wotd/index.pperl?date=19990202.
6. 691 Voting Rights Act of 1965: 42 UCS 1973b.
7. McClanahan, *supra,* p. 18.
8. Ibid., pp. 18–19.

9. Ibid., p. 19.
10. Ibid.
11. Ibid.
12. Ibid., p. 21.
13. This quotation appears several places on the Internet, none of which cite any original authority.
14. *The Annals of America, Vol. 3*, *supra*, p. 606.

Chapter Six

Executive Reform

Of all the books that have been written about amending the Constitution to save the nation, the most whimsical, though not the least valuable, is *Me, the People: One Man's Selfless Quest to Rewrite the Constitution of the United States of America* by Kevin Bleyer.

An Emmy Award-winning writer for the *The Daily Show with Jon Stewart*, Bleyer spoofs everything and everybody in the American History books, but never without a tasty kernel of truth. Here is a sample:

> They also invented a means of electing our president that, to this day, confounds every political science Ph.D., historian, and armchair politico who gives it a moment's thought. And they did so merely because one man—a man who, it should be noted, refused to sign the Declaration of Independence and who had been absent for much of the Constitutional Convention—stepped in at the eleventh hour to see what he had been missing. John Dickinson, who had been sick (or at least claimed to be so) and therefore absent for much of late August and into September, joined the committee just as they were about to endorse a proposal to give the Congress—not we the people—the power to elect the president. Dickinson, aghast, wondered aloud how they had come to such an antidemocratic conclusion—not that he had been around to help. He warned them that the "powers which we have agreed to vest in the President were so many and so great"—to command armies, to make treaties, to appoint ambassadors—that the people would never ratify, let alone support, a plan featuring such a scheme "unless they themselves would be more immediately concerned in [the president's] election. These are Americans, after all, They'll want to have a say. Murmurs of agreement began to ripple through the committee, and soon peg-legged Gouverneur Morris insisted they all "sit down again, and converse further on the subject." It was then that James Madison took out a Pen and Paper, and sketched out a Mode of Electing the President that involved a complex system of representatives elected by the people for the sole purpose of casting their vote for the president. It was a ridiculous Band-

> Aid applied only to assuage the increasingly stubborn delegates, who couldn't complain about it largely because they couldn't understand it. It was the least bad option. It was the Electoral College.[1]

With that ambivalent launching, it should be no surprise that the Electoral College remains one of the most controverted provisions of the United States Constitution. Like many of the conflicts confronted by the Philadelphia convention, the manner of choosing the President involved a compromise between large, populous states and small states with fewer inhabitants.

It also involved a more subtle compromise. On the subject of the presidency, delegates were largely divided between those who had confidence in the people and those who were leery of popular sovereignty. In addition to Shay's Rebellion in Massachusetts, there were a number of other incidents in which mobs of people were acting riotously.

Just two weeks before the delegates were to meet in Philadelphia, and less than five blocks from their meeting place, a woman known as "Widow Korbmacher" had been attacked by a crowd accusing her of being a witch. In mid-July, while the delegates were in session, she was attacked again, stoned by the mob, and died of her injuries.[2]

Some delegates were leery of letting the general public elect the President. They preferred a system in which the President was elected by the Congress. They saw the federal government as one controlled by the people, through an elected Congress, with the President being the agent of Congress, charged with the duty of carrying out its orders and wishes. In many respects this would have been similar to the parliamentary systems in England and Canada.

Others, like James Wilson, wanted a President who would be a "man of all the people." He believed that a popularly elected President would be less likely to favor his home state of section of the country. Wilson and others wanted a strong and independent chief executive, more like a king than a prime minister.

By requiring the election of Electors with the sole responsibility of voting for the President, Madison was able to assuage those who wanted an elected Chief Executive. By including the number of senators in the computation of electors, he threw a bone to the small states, and to those who did not trust the general public to choose a chief executive. In theory, this two step selection process would be insulation against the selection of demagogues. As a practical matter, in an age of mass communication, the Electoral College will mirror the popular will, especially if the House of Representatives is enlarged.

It is, of course, theoretically possible for a candidate to win a majority in the Electoral College without winning a majority of the actual popular vote. It has happened four times: John Quincy Adams lost by 44,804 votes to

Andrew Jackson in 1824; Rutherford B. Hayes lost by 264,292 to Samuel J. Tilden in 1876; Benjamin Harrison lost by 95,713 votes to Grover Cleveland in 1888, and finally George Bush polled 543,816 fewer votes than Al Gore in 2000.

Popular election of the President is an issue that commands overwhelming majority support across America. Still, it has never been the subject of a constitutional amendment proposed by the Congress. Nor is that likely to happen. In order to muster a two-thirds majority vote in the Senate, at least a few small states would have to support it. They are not inclined to do so.

Of course, should the number of representatives in the House be substantially increased, the consequence of including the number of Senators in the Electoral College equation would be diluted, but it still would not assure that the President would always have a popular majority for two reasons; third party candidates, and winner-take-all legislation.

There remains the possibility of a third party candidate corralling enough voters to deny a majority to either of the major party candidates. This is a lingering problem with what has become known as "the two party system." Many Americans believe that the two party system, so called, is an official and legal component of American governance. They would be surprised to learn that there is nothing in the constitution about a two party system.

In fact, as we have seen, George Washington warned against the spirit of partisanship. He was not alone among the founders to entertain that opinion. The division of the electorate into two major political parties is not constitutional, nor strictly speaking is it legal. State laws that authorize party primaries typically permit any group of people to form a party. However they sometimes limit ballot space to parties that garnered a significant percentage of the popular vote in the last election. Those rules favor the so-called "major" parties.

In recent years much public attention has been given to the "primary season," the nearly year-long period during which the two major political parties select their presidential candidate in state by state partisan primary elections. While it is true that third party candidates are eligible to seek party nominations, it is also true that they can seek a separate place on the final ballot in November.

Perhaps the only constitutional method of eliminating the threat that a third party candidacy might prevent a majority decision would be the establishment of a nationwide presidential primary, which would pare the field down to two candidates.

The other impediment to a guaranteed majority winner is the prevalence of winner-take-all legislation in the states. Because of these laws, large blocks of electoral votes can be won or lost by a tiny margin. Polls have indicated that as many as 80 percent of the American people favor popular election of the President. Even so, only Maine and Nebraska have awarded electoral votes to candidates by congressional districts The rest of the states give all of their electoral votes to the candidate who carries the state.

As a result of this kind of legislation, many states' electoral votes are assured to one or the other of the two major political parties. There is no need to count the votes in New York or Illinois. Their electoral votes will go to the candidate of the Democratic Party. Texas or Oklahoma will give their electoral votes to the Republican. Many voters in solidly red or blue states simply don't bother to vote. More importantly, the parties don't make a major or expensive effort to turn out their supporters in states that are conceded to the opposition.

Predictable results will be posted by perhaps thirty-three to thirty-six of the fifty states. Only the remaining fourteen to seventeen states are regarded as "swing" states, whose voting majority might choose either of the candidates. This factor, this 'swing state' phenomenon, causes the major candidates to concentrate their electoral efforts in the swing states. Well over 90 percent of the campaign funds, and the major portion of the candidates' time and attention is directed to these few states.

These facts of political life substantially affect the outcome of the popular vote. Why would New York Republicans bother to vote? They have nothing to say about electing the President. Many of them know it, and they simply don't bother to go to the polls. In 2000, George Bush lost the popular vote to Al Gore by about half a million votes. The vote in the state of New York was 4,113,791 for Gore and 2,405,676 for Bush. Another half million Republicans in the Empire State would not have affected the electoral vote, but would have made a difference in the popular vote.

It remains to be seen whether a constitutional amendment affecting the Electoral College, that might emanate from a convention of elected delegates, would have sufficient widespread support to muster ratification in three quarters of the states. There is, however, another route to change the system, that is gaining some traction. The National Popular Vote initiative is an attempt to circumvent the Electoral College without amending the Constitution. It involves persuading the legislatures of states having a total of 270 Electoral votes—enough to elect a President—to adopt statutes providing that the state's electoral votes will go to the candidate receiving the greater number of popular votes nationwide, regardless of how the candidate may have fared in that state.

At this writing the movement has garnered support of the legislatures in states having a combined total of 136 electoral votes, about 50.4 percent of the total needed. The states already agreeing to the National Popular Vote program are: Rhode Island, Vermont, Maryland, Washington, Illinois, New Jersey, District of Columbia, Massachusetts, California, and Hawaii.

Beyond the matter of how Presidents are elected, there are a number of issues respecting the Executive branch of the national government that should be articulated in the context of a serious effort to amend the constitution as contemplated by Article V.

CABBAGES AND KINGS

In his seminal work, *The Once and Future King: The Rise of Crown Government in America*, Canadian-born F.H. Buckley, a Foundation Professor at George Mason University Law School and former visiting Olin Fellow at the University of Chicago Law School has shattered just about every myth surrounding American government, and our constitution.

Buckley, who has taught at the Sorbonne in Paris and on the McGill Faculty of Law in Montreal, describes the American version of monarchy in these words:

> Republican ceremonies in the United States, centered around the president, mimic those of a royalty in a monarchy. In place of a coronation there is a presidential inauguration , the departing president accompanying the new president from the White House to the Capitol, followed by the oath of office, the departure of the former president by helicopter from the Capitol's East Front, the inaugural address from the West Front, the parade down Pennsylvania Avenue, the prayer services and balls. In place of the Royal Family there is the First Family. In place of "God Save the Queen" there is "Hail to the Chief." A distinguished career merits a presidential medal; a national tragedy requires a presidential speech.[3]

Buckley goes on to note that the trappings of royalty don't come cheap. Britain spends about $60 million a year to support its royal family. By contrast, he notes, President Obama's 2010 vacation to Mumbai cost the American taxpayers a reputed $200 million a day.[4]

Of course, the real danger associated with the American fascination with and adulation of the celebrity of the chief executive is the assumption on all sides that the trappings of divinity carry with them the divine right to rule. To a monarch, the people are not citizens, they are subjects. Sovereignty resides in the king, not in the people. There are no limits to the powers of a king. He rules by decree. What he says is the law and must be obeyed. His every command is backed by the full military force of the realm.

In their feisty expose, *Who Killed the Constitution?* Thomas E. Woods Jr. and Kevin R. C. Gutzman detail President Harry S. Truman's April 1952 seizure of the American steel mills. In a radio broadcast on April 8, Truman attempted to justify his action by an appeal to "the constitution and laws of the United States" and his powers "as President of the United States and Commander-in-Chief of the armed forces."[5]

The twentieth century hosted an almost uninterrupted march in the nation's Capital toward what can only be called the Imperial Presidency. From

Teddy Roosevelt's "Bully Pulpit," to Woodrow Wilson's call to "visionary leadership," Franklin Roosevelt's "New Deal" and Harry Truman's "Fair Deal" to John Kennedy's "Ask Not . . .," Ronald Reagan's "City on a Hill" to Barack Obama's "Hope and Change," the office of President of the United States has expanded its writ and multiplied its influence exponentially.

Woodrow Wilson might well be characterized as the godfather of the imperial presidency. He believed that the Constitution's system of checks and balances was Newtonian, that is based on the idea that there are certain fixed principles or postulates that are imbedded in human nature and need to be taken into account in the constitution. He disagreed with that theory, feeling that human life was better understood in a Darwinian context: everybody is different and everything changes.

Wilson concluded that it is possible to write about Presidents, but not about the presidency. He viewed the constitution as a sort of Magna Carta; an historic statement of aspirations, which only has such effect as people choose to give it from generation to generation. Presidents, he believed, are both the legal and the political leaders of their parties and the nation, and while he conceded that such conduct was "deeply immoral," he nevertheless opined that a president could, if he wished, substitute his own orders for acts of Congress.

Given those notions by an illustrious predecessor, it is little wonder that Barack Obama can announce with a straight face that he has a pen and a telephone with which to do what Congress won't do.

Most dramatically, and chillingly, the presence of the "big red button" in the Oval Office with which the President of the United States is reputedly able to launch instantaneous, atomic Armageddon lends an eerie credibility to the description of the American President as "the most powerful man in the world."

This attitude reflects itself in two important ways. First, there is the milieu of the Oval Office. Heightened security, inspired by terror attacks, has multiplied the magnificent isolation of the President and his family and the minute details of protection that accompany him and his family at every moment.

No monarch enjoys a palace more carefully protected than the White House. No Middle Eastern potentate travels with a larger entourage of bodyguards, servants, and aides de camp.

In this century, largely because of the 9/11 attacks on New York City and the Pentagon, the presidencies of George W. Bush and Barack Obama have taken on much of the aura of a Mafia Don. The American people are pragmatic to a fault. To most of them, whatever must be done can and should be done.

Publication of the fact that the President maintains a "kill" list of reputed "public enemies," the most notorious eliminations of whom by military drones inspires barely a yawn in the national newsrooms, confirms the chilling fact that the American public has, by dint of repeated acquiescence, confirmed that the President of the United States enjoys the same power over life and death as did the English monarchs of the fourteenth century.

It cannot be denied that this extra-constitutional presidential option is at least partially a function of the fact that the United States has been intermittently at war ever since it was last declared by Congress in 1941, and continuously involved in active warfare for the last thirteen years.

No one disputes the plain words of Article I, Section 8 of the Constitution, which empower the Congress to declare war. Of course those who would augment the words of the Constitution with "amendment by disobedience" will argue that the Constitution does not prohibit the President from making war without a declaration by Congress.

Indulge me now, while I cast out a bit of lawyer talk. *Expressio unius est exclusio alterius* is a Latin expression, which means "the expression of one thing is the exclusion of other things."[6] It is a maxim used to decipher the meaning of written documents. By telling us that the Congress has the power to declare war, the Constitution clearly infers that no one else has that power. There would be no need to specify that Congress has that power if, in fact, the President, or any other official of the national government were intended to have the power as well.

The reason that declaring war was left to the Congress is apparent upon reflection. War is serious business. It places the very existence of a nation at risk. It summons the efforts, the lives and fortunes of every citizen. It is the function of the Congress to speak for the people.

In his Farewell Address, George Washington cautioned the American people to protect the public credit. He advised the nation to discharge in peacetime those financial burdens necessarily taken on during time of war, so as not to burden our progeny with obligations we ourselves should bear.

Interesting that Washington expected that the nation would have to borrow in time of war. That comment reflected his disapproval, held in concert with almost all of the Founding Fathers, of standing armies. The Founders viewed standing armies as a threat to the liberties of the people.

The anti-militaristic disposition of the founders was reflected in the second amendment's protection of the people's right to bear arms, as well as in the sentence in Section 8 of Article I immediately after the grant of war power to Congress. It permits the national legislature:

"To raise and support Armies, but no appropriation of Money to that Use shall be for a longer Term than two years."

It would surely be of no surprise to the Father of our Country to learn that his beloved nation has run up a national debt of $17 trillion during a period of seventy years in which the government was either at war or preparing for war.

PAX AMERICANA

The terror of Hiroshima and Nagasaki not only ended the Second World War, it also thrust the United States into the role of guardian of the peace of the planet. The Pax Americana is not maintained without an unsustainable financial burden. The United States has military boots on the ground in more than 150 countries around the world. True, about 122 of them have a garrison of less than 100 people. These are the others:

- Japan, 50,341
- Germany, 40,304
- South Korea, 28,500
- Kuwait, 12,139
- Italy, 10,971
- United Kingdom, 9,501
- Bahrain, 2,977
- Kyrgyzstan, 2,798
- Turkey, 1,519
- Spain, 1,462
- Belgium, 1,187

Portugal, Qatar, British Indian Ocean Territory, United Arab Emirates, Saudi Arabia, Thailand, Egypt, South Africa, Australia, and Singapore, have less than 1,000 GIs each.[7]

This detour into the realm of statistics seemed to be needed in order to demonstrate that the nature of the Presidency has been deeply affected by the course of history. The Preamble to the Constitution of the United States recites, among our six national purposes, that our nation was formed "to provide for the common defence [*sic*]."

Maintaining the peace and good order of the world is not mentioned. Surely it is not embraced within the idea of the "common defense." On August 8, 1945, the United States dropped an atom bomb on Nagasaki, Russia declared war on Japan, and President Harry Truman signed the United Nation's Charter. The war would be over in a week. The world was optimistic that a new era of peace was about to dawn.

It hasn't. What has happened is that the United States of America has taken on the job of policing the world. Our Commander in Chief has become the Chief of Police of the planet. Deploying Yankee boots all around the globe has become a central function of the Oval Office.

In the rush to become the leader of the free world, the people of the United States have lost sight of the wise counsel of our forebears. Harken to James Madison:

> Of all the enemies to public liberty war is, perhaps, the most to be dreaded, because it comprises and develops the germ of every other. War is the parent of armies; from these proceed debts and taxes; and armies, and debts, and taxes are the known instruments for bringing the many under the dominion of the few. In war, too, the discretionary power of the Executive is extended; its influence in dealing out offices, honors, and emoluments is multiplied; and all the means of seducing the minds, are added to those of subduing the force, of the people. The same malignant aspect in republicanism may be traced in the inequality of fortunes, and the opportunities of fraud, growing out of a state of war, and in the degeneracy of manners and of morals engendered by both. No nation could preserve its freedom in the midst of continual warfare. [8]

The case for Presidential war power has been stated in many academic and media publications. Rather typical is the didactic pronouncement of Professor John Yoo of the Law School at the University of California at Berkeley.

Yoo maintains that the President of the United States has the constitutional authority to send American troops into battle any time, anywhere, for whatever reason, or no reason at all, on his own authority, without the consent and without consultation with either House of the Congress.

His principal argument is that Presidents have done it in the past. In this approach he echoes the view of many academics who believe the constitution is archaic and no longer means what it says. Here is what Professor Yoo says:

Throughout our history, neither presidents nor Congresses have acted under the belief that the Constitution requires a declaration of war before the U.S. can conduct military hostilities abroad.

We have used force abroad more than 100 times but declared war in only five cases: the War of 1812, the Mexican-American and Spanish-American Wars, and World Wars I and II.

Without any congressional approval, presidents have sent forces to battle Indians, Barbary pirates, and Russian revolutionaries, to fight North Korean and Chinese communists in Korea, to engineer regime changes in South and Central America, and to prevent human rights disasters in the Balkans. [9]

Other conflicts, such as the 1991 Persian Gulf War, the 2001 invasion of Afghanistan, and the 2003 Iraq War, received legislative "authorization" but not declarations of war.

The practice of presidential initiative, followed by congressional acquiescence, has spanned both Democratic and Republican administrations and reaches back from President Obama to Presidents Abraham Lincoln, Thomas Jefferson, and George Washington.

As Alexander Hamilton wrote in Federalist #74, "The direction of war implies the direction of the common strength, and the power of directing and employing the common strength forms a usual and essential part in the definition of the executive authority."

Presidents should conduct war, he wrote:

> because they could act with "decision, activity, secrecy, and dispatch." In perhaps his most famous words, Hamilton wrote: "Energy in the executive is a leading character in the definition of good government. . . . It is essential to the protection of the community against foreign attacks."[10]

Professor Yoo tries to make Alexander Hamilton's argument in favor of the President *conducting* a war into an argument that Hamilton thought the President should have the power to *initiate* warfare.

The good professor has misconstrued Mr. Hamilton. Here is what Hamilton wrote in Federalist #69:

> Secondly. The President is to be commander-in-chief of the army and navy of the United States. In this respect his authority would be nominally the same with that of the king of Great Britain, but in substance much inferior to it. It would amount to nothing more than the supreme command and direction of the military and naval forces, as first General and admiral of the Confederacy; while that of the British king extends to the declaring of war and to the raising and regulating of fleets and armies, all which, by the Constitution under consideration, would appertain to the legislature.[11]

Granting Professor Yoo's point, shared by so many Americans, that modern society requires prompt and effective response to dangers and threats to security, more flexible and more immediate than the powers envisioned by the founders, the conclusion that no amendment of the constitution is necessary is diametrically opposed to the truth.

If, indeed the passage of time and the introduction of technology have made our constitution arcane in any respect, the remedy is not to ignore it. The remedy is to fix it. That is what our forebears intended. If the constitution is to say what it means and mean what it says, we cannot simply shrug our shoulders and say, "Well, we don't abide by that part of it anyway."

If the President of the United States is to be authorized to commit the fortunes and the blood of the American people to the attainment of some geopolitical objective, our constitution should say so, and it should also say when she cannot do so.

It is a subject, which ought to be on the agenda of the convention. The constitution requires the President to seek the advice and consent of the Senate when appointing the principal officers of the national government. Would it be too cumbersome, would it not be prudent, to require her to turn to the same counsel before putting American men and women in harms way halfway around the world?

The Senate is, after all, supposed to represent the states. Senators have long, staggered terms precisely so that they can be expected to acquire expertise and experience in government. They must be consulted on treaties or peace, why not also on starting wars?

THE IMPERIAL PRESIDENCY

Section 1 of Article II of the Constitution says this:

> The President shall, at stated Times, receive for his Services, a Compensation, which shall neither be increased nor diminished during the Period for which he shall have been elected, and he shall not receive within that period any other Emolument from the United States or any of them.

This surely is a provision that has been honored in the breach more than any other. Consider:

1. The President and his family are provided a luxurious home with a full staff of domestic servants.
2. The President and his family—and guests—are welcome to vacation at Camp David.
3. The President has at his beck and call a magnificent airplane known as Air Force One, which he uses to transport himself and his family on a vacation in Hawaii, including a special round trip to allow his wife to stay a few more days. That same aircraft can be summoned to transport the President and the First Lady to New York City to attend the theater.
4. After service as President of the United States, he will continue to receive a salary for life, personal and family security, transportation, an office, and support staff.

The detailing of these prerequisites should not be taken as any criticism. The office of President of the United States is surely an awesome and exhausting responsibility, and whatever is provided by way of comfort, convenience, and security is well-deserved and reflects the respect and gratitude of the nation.

But none of it is consistent with the stingy words of the national charter. If the constitution does not specify what emoluments the President shall be entitled to, there is always the possibility, indeed the likelihood, that some future president would expand his demands beyond what might be viewed as reasonable and appropriate.

President Clinton's dalliance with an intern should remind us that potentates through history generally exhibit an above average libido. Considering John Kennedy's oft whispered-about mischief it is not beyond the realm of conjecture that some future occupant of the White House might wish to avail himself of emoluments somewhat beyond those generally conceded to be appropriate for the Commander in Chief.

The point is simply that the constitution should say what it means and mean what it says.

THE RIGHT TO KILL

History is replete with examples of monarchs who dispatched their political opponents with or without the benefit of trumped up charges and railroaded trials. From King David's removal of his girlfriend's husband to Henry VIII's beheading of Anne and Catherine to Hitler's extermination of millions of Jews and Syngman Rhee's slaughter of political dissidents, the disposition of heads of state to enhance their security or comfort by killing people is a sad truth of human history.

Macbeth murders King Duncan, and becomes the King of Scotland. Before the final curtain, MacDuff has beheaded Macbeth and succeeded to the throne. No need for term limits back then. Indeed killing people has a long and storied history in the politics of human governance.

Louis XVI, Benito Mussolini, and Muammar Gaddafi are all rather well-known examples of leaders mortally removed from office by their constituents. Some victims, like Abraham Lincoln and John Kennedy, are seen as martyrs. Many others are hardly noticed.

Fifteen political leaders were assassinated in the United States in the ninteenth century. Seventeen more, including John and Robert Kennedy and Martin Luther King, were murdered in the twentieth century.

We're off to a strong start in the twenty-first century. Five American politicians have been killed in the first decade:

Derwin Brown (a Georgia sheriff-elect, murdered on orders of the man he defeated), James Davis (New York City councilman), Bill Gwatney (chairman of the Arkansas Democratic Party), Mike Swoboda (mayor of Kirkwood, Missouri), and John Thornton (mayor of Washington Park, Illinois).

All were condemned to death for the crime of aspiring to public service. Of course voting with guns and knives goes both ways. Bashar al-Assad has reputedly slaughtered tens of thousands of his constituents in a frantic effort to stay in office. There is a substantial body of literature in the United States which presumes that the Counter Intelligence Agency, popularly known as the CIA, and frequently dubbed "the company" is, from time to time, expected to 'eliminate' dangerous enemies of the nation.

Matt Damon as "Jason Bourne" romps through a series of CIA shoot-ups; Clint Eastwood, Mel Gibson, and the Governator, Arnold Schwarzenegger, get in their licks with AK47s, and the peace and prosperity of the land is saved from the bad guys. Again.

My predecessor as Chief Justice of Michigan, a folksy Dutchman, used to say that the first issue in every murder trial is, "Should the deceased have wont?" No doubt, in the court of public opinion, the moral dimension of homicide is determined in just about that way.

Far too many Americans believe that the President of the United States has the power of life and death. His writ runs around the world, wherever a drone can land. Osama bin Laden had it coming. The Navy Seals are heroes. The President is applauded on both sides of the aisle. He taught those al-Qaeda guys a lesson. Now we don't have to worry about them any more. Do we? Or have we created a martyr and insured the continuation of bin Laden's efforts to terrorize Christiandom. Perhaps we should assume that the Benghazi massacre was just a ruckus about an offensive anti-Muslim video. Otherwise someone might just suggest that it was retribution for the offing of bin Laden. And, of course, if it was, then in the eyes of the Muslim world, we had it coming. In the insane tradition of the middle east, it is now our turn to kill somebody.

Too many Americans believe that constitutional authority depends on the success of the outcome. "Should the deceased have went?"

Abdulrahman al-Awlaki was the son of Anwar al-Awlaki. The father was killed in Yemen by an American drone. An American citizen who reputedly renounced his citizenship, the father was known to be an advisor to Nidal Hasan, who slaughtered a dozen Americans at Fort Hood.

The son, a sixteen-year-old American citizen had gone to Yemen trying to find his father. He was killed by another drone two weeks after his father, along with a carload of other teenagers who had the misfortune of having lunch with al-Awlaki. Former White House Press Secretary, Robert Gibbs, defended the killing by saying that the boy should have had a more responsible father.

Even the mainstream *Washington Post* has reported that the administration has a secret "kill list." Too many Americans are content to think that when someone is killed by a drone, "they must have had it coming, or we wouldn't have killed them."

I cannot subscribe to that kind of thinking. I suggest that it is time for a national debate on the issue of Presidential powers. Does the President of the United States have the power of life and death? Should he have that authority?

It is campy to say that "the buck stops here" in the Oval Office. But how is it that the buck ever gets there in the first place? Who recommends names for the kill list? And why?

I would endorse a constitutional amendment like this:

> Except in the prosecution of a war duly declared by the Congress, the President shall not order nor authorize the killing of any human being without the prior advice and consent of the Senate.

In any case, I believe that such an amendment ought to be debated at an Article V Convention.

THE BUREAUCRACY

There is no more baneful subject in the history of the United States of America than bureaucracy. Bureaucracy is variously described as "government organization," "the civil service," "the executive branch," or simply "the government."

It encompasses some 2.8 million employees, who are supposed to be selected on the basis of merit, competence, or expertise. They are expected to do their assigned work free from political influence and free from domination by private corporate or moneyed interests.

Many bureaucrats are appointed by the President. To that extent, the bureaucracy is a spoils system in which the President and his party can reward those who have helped in political campaigns, and engage those who can be expected to help in future campaigns. Through the years, there have been attempts to ameliorate this aspect of government service. Civil service examinations are one means of trying to hire on the basis of merit, and the Hatch Act prohibits federal employees from most blatant political activity.

Still, the ingenuity and self interest of mankind being what they are, ways can always be found to harness the mighty horsepower of a federal paycheck in the cause of partisan prosperity. Perhaps the most egregious mischief invented in the back halls of bureaucracy is the practice of awarding bonuses to salaried employees.

That program came to light recently when it was revealed that supervisors of the Internal Revenue staff, who were giving extra scrutiny to the exempt status applications of Tea Party and other conservative organizations, received performance bonuses amounting to as much as $100,000.

The very notion of a bonus—a discretionary payment of additional compensation for services already performed—is anathema in the setting of government civil service. Supposedly given for efforts over and above the requirements of the position, the decision to award a bonus entices the decision-maker to reward partisan bias in the performance of administrative duties.

It is inherently contradictory to hire an applicant based on merit demonstrated by a civil service examination, and then allow her supervisor to incentivize the way the job is performed by the anticipation of added compensation. And, of course, the fact that some of these bonuses have to be approved by the President only adds to the political overtones.

To the average citizen, the national bureaucracy is a monolithic monstrosity, incomprehensible, intractable, immovable, and frightening. It represents the twenty-first century's most realistic threat to personal liberty, economic freedom and political democracy.

In general, the bureaucracy can be divided into four categories: 1) Cabinet departments, 2) independent executive agencies, 3) independent regulatory agencies, and 4) federal corporations.

At present there are fourteen Cabinet Departments. The Cabinets Departments are the first level of the executive organizational chart. They are led by Cabinet Secretaries who are appointed by the President with the advice and consent of the Senate. They serve at the pleasure of the President. In addition to these fourteen offices, there are seven more so-called "cabinet level" offices or agencies, that have a seat at Cabinet meetings.

Independent executive and regulatory agencies are usually operated by a board or commission that is appointed by and directly responsible to the President. Federal corporations are technically not part of the government at all, but are private entities chartered by the Congress for a particular purpose. Officers of these companies may be appointed by the President or by their corporate boards.

The Internet lists over 525 federal agencies, administrations, boards, bureaus, commissions, councils, centers, committees, colleges, departments, offices, and programs. Redundancy is epidemic. Every one of those 525 phone numbers will connect you with a fiefdom presided over by someone who is both well-connected and dependent on his or her government paycheck.

Sorting out this morass of economically entangled humanity will take a generation of relentless down sizing, but it can be done, and it will be done if the decision-makers in the United States Congress are truly representative of the American people, and the President willingly or reluctantly cooperates.

Just to understand the nature of this bureaucratic beast, consider this: during the administration of our first President George Washington, the national government employed fifty civilians. They had no electronic devices, nor even manual typewriters with which to work. They had a great deal to do, what with literally organizing the government from ground zero. Those fifty civilians represented about one employee for every 60,000 people in the nation.

Certainly with modern technology human productivity has advanced incrementally. Still, the workforce in our national government today represents one employee for every 100 Americans. That means you and ninety-nine other good folks in your town have got to chip in and pick up the tab for one bureaucrat in Washington, DC. Not to mention who pays the soldiers and sailors.

The Congress is not likely to bite the bullet and actually do something about the bloated bureaucracy. For one thing there is the phenomenon known as the "iron triangle." It refers to a situation in which a regulatory agency, a congressional committee or subcommittee and interested corporate lobbyists work on a friendly, informal, and exclusionary basis. Let's consider the case of a hypothetic American Banana Commission (ABC) ostensibly created by Congress to help Americans grow, sell, buy, and eat bananas.

There are three points on the iron triangle: the regulators on the Banana Commission, the representatives of the banana growers, and the members of the powerful House banana committee. They meet for lunch often, and usually the talk turns to—you guessed it—bananas. Out of these frequent and cordial meetings will come administrative rules that: 1) require banana growers to be certified by the National Banana Growers Association 2) prohibit the bulk sale of bananas for less than the RWPB (Reasonable Wholesale Price of Bananas) and 3) require all military establishments and schools participating in federal nutritional supplement subsidies to provide MDBC (Minimum Daily Banana Calories) for all soldiers and students.

The banana growers who belong to the NBGA are certainly going to defend the ABC against any reformers bent on downsizing the national government. So too, are the members of the House Banana Committee, whose campaign funds are enhanced by donations from NBGA members. The bureaucrats at the ABC obviously don't want their sinecure to be phased out. Fortunately for them, their close working relationship with the committee members will hold them in good stead on the floor of the House.

What exactly can be done about the bloated federal bureaucracy? Mark Levin has a suggestion. Here it is:

> SECTION 1: All federal departments and agencies shall expire if said departments and agencies are not individually authorized in stand-alone reauthorization bills every three years by a majority vote of the House of Representatives and the Senate.
>
> SECTION 2: All Executive Branch regulations exceeding an economic burden of $100 million, as determined jointly by the Government Accountability Office and the Congressional Budget Office, shall be submitted to a permanent Joint Committee of Congress, hereafter the Congressional Delegation Oversight Committee, for review and approval prior to their implementation.
>
> SECTION 3: The Committee shall consist of seven members of the House of Representatives, four chosen by the Speaker and three chosen by the Minority Leader; and seven members of the Senate, four chosen by the Majority Leader and three chosen by the Minority Leader. No member shall serve on the Committee beyond a single three-year term.
>
> SECTION 4: The Committee shall vote no later than six months from the date of the submission of the regulation to the Committee. The Committee shall make no change to the regulation, either approving or disapproving the regulation by majority vote as submitted.
>
> SECTION 5: If the Committee does not act within six months from the date of the submission of the regulation to the Committee, the regulation shall

> be considered disapproved and must not be implemented by the Executive branch.

As brilliant as Mr. Levin is, and I am persuaded he is very brilliant, his suggested constitutional amendment respecting the bureaucracy suggests the absence of a devil's advocate.

First off, he gives the Congress three years to reinvent the government. Anyone who has observed the continual re-extension of the so-called debt ceiling should be able to see that a dysfunctional Congress can kick a project as massive as reinventing the government down the street almost indefinitely. The daunting task of reauthorizing agencies and commissions individually would assure that none of them would be carefully examined. Wholesale reauthorization would most certainly occur.

Section 2 makes the mistake of using a dollar amount. That is not a wise thing to put in a constitution. Witness the seventh amendment protection of twenty-five dollar jury trials. Then it goes on to give duties to two nonconstitutional bodies—the Government Accountability Office and the Congressional Budget Office—either one of which could be dissolved by Congress in a heartbeat. Finally, imitating the bureaucracy, Levin would create the Congressional Delegation Oversight Committee (CDOC?), adding yet another unpronounceable acronym to the Bureaucratic lexicon.

In Section 3, Levin would embed the "two party system," so dreaded by George Washington and the other Founders, into the Constitution. Minority and Majority are terms they never used.

I am not one to nitpick for its own sake. It has always been my rule that, if you haven't a better idea don't criticize. That said, I offer a suggestion that I believe would warrant serious consideration in an Article V constitutional convention.

BUREAUCRACY REFORM AMENDMENTS

> SECTION 1: Upon petition of any thirty members of both Houses of the Congress, the ayes and nays upon the continued existence of any administrative entity created by Act of Congress shall forthwith be taken without debate, and if the vote shall fail of a majority in both Houses, the entity shall be forthwith disbanded, and its employees separated with one year's pay as compensation for severance.
>
> SECTION 2: Upon the petition of any ten members of both Houses of the Congress, the ayes and nays shall forthwith be taken without debate upon any published administrative regulation, and if it shall fail of a majority in both Houses, it shall be removed from the Federal Register and all actions taken in pursuance thereof shall be null and void.
>
> SECTION 3: Congress shall not charter any private corporation, nor appropriate any monies for such purpose, nor authorize the treasury to invest in

> or subsidize any private corporation or enterprise, except as authorized by Section 8 of Article I for Post Offices and Post Roads.

Assuming that this amendment would have a salutary effect on the bloated bureaucracy, it still could not be presumed that the ship of state would be as sleek and yar as an America's Cup champion. Even the most sanguine estimate of what might be accomplished by a bully spate of ayes and nays would have to concede that a substantial majority of those 500 odd bureaucratic domains would survive.

What to do with hundreds of thousands of civilian government employees? How can the bureaucracy be made more efficient, more effective, more responsive? And smaller?

Step one: sell the corporations. There are seventeen specially chartered federal corporations at the present time. The only one that can be said to be contemplated by the Constitution is the U.S. Post Office. All the others should be sold and made to compete in the open market.

While engaging in business of one kind or another, these corporations have been regarded as public utilities or public service entities. Each has its own governing board. Their employees and officers are not federal government employees. Since each has a stream of revenue, they should be required to meet their own costs in competition with the private sector.

But then what? Even assuming the federal corporations are disposed of, much remains to be done to untangle the bureaucratic labyrinth that remains. I am sure it must exist somewhere, government work being what it is, but I have been unable to locate an organizational chart of the Executive Branch of the federal government

Undaunted, I advance this suggestion, which, incidentally, I believe would be an appropriate item on a constitutional convention agenda: Resolved: that the constitution should outline the basic structure of the Executive Department.

Section 2 of Article II of the Constitution says this:

> The President shall be Commander in Chief of the Army and Navy of the United States, and of the Militia of the several States, when called into the actual Service of the United States; he may require the Opinion, in writing, of the principal Officer in each of the executive Departments, upon any Subject relating to the Duties of their respective Offices, and he shall have a Power to grant Reprieves and pardons for Offenses against the United States, except in Cases of Impeachment.

Skimpy as the evidence may be, the Constitution nonetheless establishes 1) that there are to be executive Departments and 2) that each department shall have a principal Officer and 3) that the principal Officers of the executive

Departments shall report directly to the President of the United States. The word 'cabinet' appears nowhere in the Constitution.

To begin at the beginning therefore, the organizational chart would show the President at the top and directly under her or him would be a bar on which the titles of the principal officers of the executive Departments would appear. This brings us to the main policy question that should be decided upon by the people of the United States and included in the Constitution:

How many departments should there be?

Cannot the work of the Executive Branch of government be divided into a given number of segments, roughly equal in importance and the share of the President's attention they should command?

Let the Constitution define the President's cabinet, determining the number of Departments, and the jurisdiction of each Department. Let the Constitution empower the several Secretaries to be the Chief Operating Officers of their respective Departments and then require that all agencies, boards, bureaus, councils, and entities of any kind previously or thereafter created by Act of Congress shall be assigned to one of the constitutional Departments of the Executive Branch.

So here is what the Constitutional Cabinet Amendment might look like:

> SECTION 1: There shall be fifteen Departments within the Executive Branch of the United States government. The Principal Officer of each department shall be known as the Secretary, and he or she shall report directly to the President.
>
> SECTION 2: There shall be the following Departments: State, Treasury, Defense, Justice, Interior, Agriculture, Commerce, Education, Energy, Health, Security, Interior, Labor, Transportation, and Housing.
>
> SECTION 3: The Secretary of each Department shall be the Chief Operating Officer of that department, and he or she shall recommend to the President the appointment of the Directors and Officers of such agencies, councils and entities as shall be assigned to the Department, as well as the principal deputies and assistants thereof.
>
> SECTION 4: The Congress shall assign all existing agencies, bureaus, entities, organizations, offices, or councils of any sort or description to one of the Cabinet Departments, and thereafter shall create no agency within the Executive branch of government which does not report to one of the constitutional departments created herein.

No doubt this reform would trigger a great many questions and many ad hoc decisions. But like organizing a messy closet, you have to start somewhere.

NOTES

1. Kevin Bleyer, *Me The People: One Man's Selfless Quest to Rewrite the Constitution of the United States of America* (New York: Random House, 2012), p. 109.

2. F. H. Buckley, *The Once and Future King: The Rise of Crown Government in America*(New York: Encounter Books, 2014), p. 38.
3. Ibid., Page 199
4. Ibid.
5. Thomas E. Woods Jr. and Gutzman, Kevin R. C., *Who Killed the Constitution?* (New York: Three Rivers Press, 2008), p. 24.
6. http://scholar.google.com/scholar?q=expressio+unius+est+exclusio+alterius&hl=en&as_sdt=0&as_vis=1&oi=scholart&sa=X&ei=jUgKU73cPKrQsQSIyoFg&sqi=2&ved=0CCQQgQMwAA.
7. http://en.wikipedia.org/wiki/United_States_military_deployments.
8. *Letters and Other Writings of James Madison*(1865), Vol. IV, p. 491
9. John Yoo, *ABA Journal, February 1, 2012.*
10. Ibid.
11. Alexander Hamilton, Federalist #59.

Chapter Seven

Judicial Reform

The founders of our nation were keenly aware that they were doing something that had never been done before. Alexander Hamilton put it this way:

> It has frequently been remarked that it seems to have been reserved to the people of this country, by their conduct and their example, to decide the important question whether societies of men are really capable or not of establishing good government from reflection and choice, or whether they are forever destined to depend for their political constitutions on accident or force.[1]

James Madison expressed a similar view:

> The important distinction so well understood in America between a constitution established by the people and unalterable by the government, and a law established by the government and alterable by the government, seems to have been little understood and less observed in any other country.[2]

In his farewell address, President George Washington reminded his audience that the Constitution, "till changed by an explicit and authentic act of the whole people, is sacredly obligatory upon all."[3] He regarded the Constitution as a binding document made by the people, a document that could only be changed by the people.

The dream of a government established by the reflection and choice of the people, a government that can only be altered by the people, is no longer the shared vision of all Americans. No one is more responsible for disrupting that dream than the one hundred and twelve men and women who have worn the robes of Justices of the United States Supreme Court.

The eleventh Chief Justice of the United States was Charles Evans Hughes, who led the court from 1930 to 1941. Did Hughes regard the constitution as a solemn and sacred compact between the sovereign people of the United States and the government they created, that could not be altered except by the authentic and explicit act of the whole people, as George Washington told us?

Not hardly. This is what Charles Evans Hughes thought about it: "The Constitution is what the Supreme Court says it is."[4]

Felix Frankfurter was an associate justice of the Supreme Court for twenty-three years, beginning in 1939. He is remembered as a Justice who cautioned his fellow jurists to exercise judicial restraint. His opinion of the Constitution doesn't sound very restraining. He taught Harvard Law School students that "the Supreme Court IS the Constitution."[5]

Thomas McIntyre Cooley, a prolific author and professor at the University of Michigan Law School who served as justice and Chief Justice of the Michigan Supreme Court from 1864 to 1885, had this to say about the Constitution:

> A cardinal rule in dealing with written instruments is that they shall receive an unvarying interpretation, and that their practical construction is to be uniform. A constitution is not to be made to mean one thing at one time, and another at some subsequent time when the circumstances may have so changed as perhaps to make a different rule in the case seem desirable. A principal share of the benefit expected from written constitutions would be lost if the rules they established were so flexible as to bend to circumstances or be modified by public opinion. It is with special reference to the varying moods of public opinion and with a view to putting the fundamentals of government beyond their control that these instruments are framed; and there can be no such steady and imperceptible change in their rules as inheres in the principles of the common law. Those beneficent maxims of the common law which guard person and property have grown and expanded until they mean vastly more to us than they did to our ancestors, and are more minute, particular and pervading in their protections; and we may confidently look forward in the future to still further modifications in the direction of improvement. Public sentiment and action effect such changes and the courts recognize them; but a court or a legislature which should allow a change in public sentiment to influence it in giving construction to a written constitution not warranted by the intention of its founders would be justly chargeable with reckless disregard of official oath and public duty; and if its course could become a precedent, these instruments would be of little avail. The violence of public passion is quite as likely to be in the direction of oppression as in any other, and the necessity of bills of rights in our fundamental laws lies mainly in the danger that the legislature will be influenced by temporary excitements and passions among the people to adopt oppressive enactments. What a court is to do, therefore, is to declare the law as written, leaving it to the people themselves to make such changes as new circumstances may require. The meaning of the constitution is fixed when it is adopted, and it is not different at any subsequent time when a court has occasion to pass upon it.

> The object of construction, as applied to a written constitution, is to give effect to the intent of the people in adopting it. In the case of all written laws, it is the intent of the lawgiver that is enforced.[6]

Chief Justice John Marshall, in the landmark case of *Marbury v. Madison*, declared that the Supreme Court has the power, or rather the duty, to declare laws that violate the Constitution void and unenforceable.

It is a tremendous power and a sacred duty that celebrates the solemn primacy and obligatory nature of the compact made by the people, which only the people can change. But it is not the words of the Court's opinions that must be obeyed. It is the words of the Constitution that the Justices are sworn to uphold that demand obedience.

CULTURE AND THE COURT

Back in the nineteenth century, the State of Connecticut adopted a law that prohibited the use of any drug, medicinal article or instrument for the purpose of preventing conception. Wikipedia provides us with the background:

> Planned Parenthood of Southern New England got its start when Katherine Hepburn's mother, Mrs. Thomas N. Hepburn, and three of her friends, Mrs. George Day, and Mr. and Mrs. M. Toscan Bennett, met with Margaret Sanger when she came to Connecticut to address supporters and the merely curious at the Parson's Theater in Hartford. After hearing her speak, the four friends formed the Connecticut Birth Control League. The year was 1923.
>
> The use of birth control, the dissemination of information about birth control, and the dispensing of birth control supplies were illegal in Connecticut at the time. The controlling law was known as the Comstock Law, after Anthony Comstock, a clergyman, who had succeeded in getting similar laws passed throughout the country in the 1870s.
>
> Despite the efforts of the original quartet and their growing number of allies, the Connecticut legislature refused to change the Comstock Law on nine different occasions between 1923 and 1931.
>
> In spite of the law, the Birth Control league established Connecticut's first birth control center in Hartford in 1935, with Dr. Hilda Standish as its medical director. Before the end of the decade the League opened additional clinics in New Haven, Stamford, Danbury, Westport, New Britain, Greenwich, Norwalk, Bridgeport, and Waterbury.
>
> Distinguished clergy and physicians were outspoken in support of birth control. In 1935, Reverend George R. Andrews, addressing the Hartford Birth Control League, urged his listeners to "change the law if we can, but if not, then let us ignore it. The law is violated daily and the men and women of greatest intelligence and character are the chief violators. To them human welfare is more important than obedience to such obnoxious laws."
>
> Six months after it opened, police raided the Waterbury clinic. Two doctors and a nurse were arrested and their contraceptive supplies were confiscat-

> ed. In the court case that followed, attorneys for the clinic contended the Comstock Law was unconstitutional. In March, 1940, however, the Connecticut Supreme Court upheld the law.
>
> The Connecticut Committee to make Birth Control legal joined the fight. Horace D. Taft, brother of President Taft and Headmaster of the Taft School, was the general chairman of the organization.
>
> Many of those who had been active in the League became part of a mostly female "underground" to get themselves and others to the birth control clinic in Portchester, New York. The League continued to litigate against the Comstock Law, but without success. It appeared that a direct challenge would be necessary.
>
> With a test case in mind, the League opened a clinic at the corner of Whitney Avenue and Trumbull Street in New Haven in 1961. C. Lee Buxton, Chairman of the Yale University Department of Obstetrics and Gynecology, was the medical director. In November, 1961 Dr. Buxton and Estelle Griswold, the Executive Director of the League were arrested.
>
> Fowler Harper, Catherine Roraback and Professor Thomas Emerson of the Yale Law School handled the case. On December 7, 1964 the United States Supreme Court agreed to hear *Griswold v. Connecticut.* The hearings took place on March 29 and 30 of 1965. Finally, on June 7, 1965, the decision was handed down by the Supreme Court.[7]

The Griswold case was not the first time that the Comstock law was challenged in court. Previous attempts had been made to test the constitutionality of the law; however, the challenges failed on technical grounds. In *Tileston v. Ullman* (1943), a doctor and mother challenged the statute on the grounds that a ban on contraception could, in certain sexual situations, threaten the lives and well-being of patients. The Supreme Court dismissed the appeal on the grounds that the plaintiff lacked standing to sue on behalf of his patients. A second challenge to the Connecticut law was brought by a doctor as well as his patients in *Poe v. Ullman* (1961). However, the Supreme Court again voted to dismiss the appeal, on the grounds that the case was not ripe. It held that, because the plaintiffs had not been charged or threatened with prosecution, there was no actual controversy for the judiciary to resolve. So the Comstock law was still on the books in 1965 when the Griswold case reached the high court.

In the Poe case, Justice John Marshall Harlan II filed one of the most cited dissenting opinions in Supreme Court history. He argued, first of all, that the Supreme Court should have heard the case, even though there was no actual controversy between the parties as required by the Constitution. Then he went on to advocate for a broad interpretation of the due process clause. His most famous line:

> The full scope of the liberty guaranteed by the Due Process Clause cannot be found in or limited by the precise terms of the specific guarantees elsewhere provided in the Constitution. This "liberty" is not a series of isolated points

> picked out in terms of the taking of property; the freedom of speech, press, and religion; the right to keep and bear arms, the freedom from unreasonable searches and seizures; and so on. It is a rational continuum which, broadly speaking, includes a freedom from all substantial arbitrary impositions and purposeless restraints.[8]

That dissenting opinion was a welcome signal to Connecticut birth control advocates, and it convinced Estelle Griswold, executive director of the Planned Parenthood League of Connecticut, and Dr. C. Lee Buxton, a physician and professor at the Yale School of Medicine to open a birth control clinic in New Haven, Connecticut, in order to test the contraception law once again.

Shortly after the clinic was opened, Griswold and Buxton were arrested, tried, found guilty, and fined $100 each. The conviction was upheld by the Appellate Division of the Circuit Court, and by the Connecticut Supreme Court. Griswold then appealed her conviction to the Supreme Court of the United States, where her counsel argued that the Connecticut statute against the use of contraceptives was contrary to the Fourteenth Amendment to the United States Constitution, which states:

> No state shall make or enforce any law which shall abridge the privileges or immunities of citizens of the United States; nor shall any State deprive any person of life, liberty, or property, without due process of law . . . nor deny any person the equal protection of the laws[9]

The U.S. Supreme Court decision in *Griswold v. Connecticut*, 381 U.S. 479 (1965). is a celebrated case in which the Court, by a 7 to 2 vote, invalidated Connecticut's Comstock Law on the grounds that it violated the "right to marital privacy."

Although the Bill of Rights does not explicitly mention "privacy," Justice William O. Douglas wrote for the majority that the right was to be found in the "penumbras" and "emanations" of other constitutional protections. Justice Arthur Goldberg wrote a concurring opinion in which he used the Ninth Amendment to defend the Supreme Court's ruling. Justice John Marshall Harlan II also wrote a concurring opinion in which he argued that privacy is protected by the due process clause of the Fourteenth Amendment. Justice Byron White added his separate concurrence based on the due process clause.

Two Justices, Hugo Black and Potter Stewart, filed dissents. Justice Black argued that the right to privacy is to be found nowhere in the Constitution. Furthermore, he criticized the interpretations of the Ninth and Fourteenth Amendments. Justice Stewart called the Connecticut statute "an uncommonly silly law" but argued that it was nevertheless constitutional.

A penumbra is defined as the partially shaded outer region of the shadow cast by an opaque object. An emanation is an abstract, but perceptible thing that issues or originates from a source.

Since Griswold, the Supreme Court has cited the right to privacy in several rulings, most notably in *Roe v. Wade*, 410 U.S. 113 (1973), where the Court ruled that a woman's choice to have an abortion was protected as a private decision between her and her doctor and *Lawrence v. Texas*, 539 U.S. 558 (2003), a 6 to 3 ruling in which the Court struck down the sodomy law in Texas.

In the tradition of the English common law, adopted by American courts, there is a doctrine of *stare decisis*. It is a Latin phrase, that simply means, “let the decision stand.” Common law courts, which decide controversies between litigants often have no statute to guide them. They are compelled to administer justice based upon their opinion of what justice in the case requires.

Judges are not supposed to decide cases by a flip of the coin. Frequently, state constitutions will provide that the Supreme Court must state the reason for its decision in writing. One of the very best reasons for a court’s decision is that a higher court has previously decided a similar case, and so there is precedent for the decision.

But *stare decisis* is not mandatory. A later court does not have to follow precedent, although in the common law tradition, respect for a higher court and the desire to avoid further appeals will almost always prevail.

The Wikipedia article about *Lawrence v. Texas* says that the court struck down the sodomy law in Texas “and, by extension, invalidated sodomy laws in thirteen other states, making same-sex sexual activity legal in every U.S. state and territory.”

The notion that *stare decisis* gives the Supreme Court of the United States the power to create rights and declare duties which are recognized throughout the United States is nowhere to be found in the Constitution.

Article VII of the Constitution says:

> This Constitution, and the Laws of the United States which shall be made in Pursuance thereof; and all treaties made, or which shall be made, under the Authority of the United States shall be the supreme Law of the Land [10]

It does not say that decisions of the Supreme Court shall be the supreme law of the land. Abraham Lincoln gave his first inaugural address on March 4, 1861. Several States had already acted to secede from the Union. The Supreme Court’s decision in the Dred Scott case, declaring that Negroes were inferior beings unable to become citizens, was a basis for much of the support for secession. Lincoln spoke to the Dred Scott decision in these words:

> I do not forget the position assumed by some that constitutional questions are to be decided by the Supreme Court, nor do I deny that such decisions must be binding in any case upon the parties to a suit as to the object of that suit, while they are also entitled to very high respect and consideration in all parallel cases by all other departments of the Government. And while it is obviously possible that such decision may be erroneous in any given case, still the evil effect following it, being limited to that particular case, with the chance that it may be overruled and never become a precedent for other cases, can better be borne than could the evils of a different practice. At the same time, the candid citizen must confess that if the policy of the Government upon vital questions affecting the whole people is to be irrevocably fixed by decisions of the Supreme Court, the instant they are made in ordinary litigation between parties in personal actions the people will have ceased to be their own rulers, having to that extent practically resigned their Government into the hands of that eminent tribunal. Nor is there in this view any assault upon the court or the judges. It is a duty from which they may not shrink to decide cases properly brought before them, and it is no fault of theirs if others seek to turn their decisions to political purposes[11]

The Tileston case, in which the Supreme Court refused to decide the legality of the Comstock Law, was decided in 1943, twelve years after the last effort to persuade the legislature to liberalize the Connecticut law, and the Poe case, in which Justice Harlan flashed his famous signal that the court was ready, was decided in 1961, a full thirty years after the last attempt to change the law democratically.

Public opinion in the nineteenth century favored the Comstock Law. As the twentieth century dawned, women began to win the right to vote in state after state, and in 1920, the nineteenth amendment was adopted assuring women the right to vote in every state. Resistance to Comstock Laws was one of the first and natural consequences of the nineteenth amendment. Clearly, the culture was changing. But it was not changing fast enough to suit the intellectual elite. And, after all, politics is dirty business. To convince the legislature to change a statute requires campaigning among the voters, the ordinary people; the great unwashed.

How much easier it is, and tidier, and dignified, simply to go to the Supreme Court and ask the Justices to change the law. They are, after all, upright gentlemen with good intentions.

It was Daniel Webster who said:

> Good intentions will always be pleaded for every assumption of power. It is hardly too strong to say that the Constitution was made to guard the people against the dangers of good intentions. There are men in all ages who mean to govern well, but they mean to govern. They promise to be good masters, but they mean to be masters.[12]

It is no exaggeration to assert that the Supreme Court of the United States has arrogated to itself the sole and unrestrained power to dictate the culture of the entire nation. The national media expects it, condones it, and reports it. There is no place, short of a constitutional convention, to stop it.

To quote a colleague of mine on the Michigan Supreme Court: "If we do it, who is to gainsay us?"

Many Americans, particularly the young, have given up on democracy, if indeed, they ever tried it. Courts are quicker, easier to deal with, and judges are eager to earn the praise and gratitude of the people

Cases like Griswold, Lawrence, and Roe attract much public attention, and a large number of *amici curiae* ("friends of the court") briefs are filed. News media treat the court's decision as a dictate, a pronouncement of law, which is immediately final and binding on all Americans. Activists flock to the clerk's office with their amici briefs. Some even congregate on the courthouse steps in spontaneous and not-so-spontaneous demonstrations of public sentiment.

It is appropriate to ask, "Who are these oracles of wisdom and truth? Who are these elevated beings, these keepers of the covenant, these prophets of the mighty and eternal Creator of humankind, so astute and all knowing as to pronounce the true and lasting words that bring happiness, prosperity, freedom and security to all the little people throughout the land?"

THE IVY CORRIDOR

George Mason was an American patriot who participated in the 1787 convention in Philadelphia that drafted the Constitution of the United States. But he didn't sign it. Mason had a premonition. He feared that the new nation would vibrate between a monarchy and a "corrupt oppressive aristocracy."

He was not alone. Between 1787 and 1791, the entire nation was absorbed in the debate over ratification of the new charter. Fear of the abuse of centralized power was at the root of most opposition. James Madison, Alexander Hamilton, and John Jay wrote detailed arguments—lawyers would call them briefs—in favor of ratification. They became known as the Federalist Papers and they made a strong case.

But it was only an argument about what the future might hold. The true believers were confident that they had designed the best plan for the future of the American people. Perhaps George Mason and Patrick Henry of Virginia, James Winthrop of Massachusetts and Melancton Smith of New York were wrong. Perhaps they were just pessimists who would not let themselves see the silver lining.

On the other hand, it is just possible that those naysayers were sounding an alarm about what could happen, what might happen, indeed what would happen, if the people of the states became too complacent, too content, too willing to let others take the lead, make the decisions, run the country.

So here we are, 230 years later. More than 90 percent of the American people have lost confidence in the Congress. Our President openly talks about ruling the nation by executive fiat. Our Supreme Court blandly goes about the theological business of dictating the cultural mores of three hundred million people who are spread over 16 percent the inhabitable land mass of the planet Earth.

And where do these learned men and women, these modern day Pharisees come from? They march down the Ivy corridor that runs from Cambridge, Massachusetts to Washington, DC, with short stops in New Haven, Connecticut and New York City, to join the self anointed cadre of the intellectual elite, the heirs of a self-perpetuating, self-aggrandizing, self-adulating, self-promoting ruling class who see themselves as the brightest and the best, and who simply assume that everyone else in the world thinks so, too.

Let's see. All nine Justices of the United States Supreme Court were educated at Harvard, Yale, or Columbia. And the Columbia graduate was a transfer student from Harvard, where she had been on law review. The President of the United States attended Columbia University and graduated from the Harvard Law School. That's two of the three branches of our national government.

Some years ago, when I was dean of the Thomas Cooley Law School in Lansing, Michigan, I noticed that all of the law clerks in the United States Supreme Court had graduated from one of four or five law schools. I wrote a letter to then Chief Justice Warren Burger and asked if there was any way for graduates of the other 165 law schools to be considered for those important and prestigious positions.

Burger replied that his former law clerks acted as a search committee and always provided him with able candidates for clerkships. This is the same Chief Justice Burger, by the way, who wrote to Phyllis Schlafly, and said that a convention as envisioned by the founders of our nation "would be a waste of time."

I wrote and suggested that there must be a better way. Then I asked the deans of all American law schools to nominate one graduating senior they felt was outstanding, and for several years we published the "National Law School Deans List" with pictures and biographies of law graduates all across America. The Supreme Court paid no attention. They have no need for outsiders. It's an attitude that pervades our nation's capital. But it is being challenged.

There is a spirit of revolt across the land. One of its provocateurs is Jimmy Wales, the founder and proprietor of Wikipedia. Educated by his mother and grandmother in a one room schoolhouse in Alabama, Jimmy has set about providing free access to the entire knowledge base of the human race.

More and more, people are learning that in the twenty-first century, it's not who you know but what you know that counts. Diplomas don't equal knowledge, virtue, or wisdom. Jimmy is telling all the secrets. He is the ultimate whistler-blower. Can the Internet save the Republic? I think so. I certainly hope so.

THE ERVIN-CLARK DEBATE

More than forty years ago, the American Enterprise Institute sponsored a debate entitled, "Role of the Supreme Court: Adjudicator or Policy Maker." The debaters were two of the most prominent and able leaders in the nation, whose expertise on the role of the Court was unquestionable. Sam J. Ervin, Jr. was widely acknowledged to be the premiere constitutional lawyer in the U.S. Senate, where he served from 1954 to 1974. He advocated that the court's proper role is to be an adjudicator. His opponent was Ramsey Clark, son of former Supreme Court Justice Tom Clark, and himself a former Attorney General of the United States. Clark defended the idea that the Supreme Court has a policy-making function.

The published transcript of their debate begins with a forward by William J. Baroody, then-president of the American Enterprise Institute. Baroody quotes the *London Economist*, saying,

> At the first sound of a new argument over the United States Constitution and its interpretation, the hearts of Americans leap with a fearful joy. The blood stirs powerfully in their veins and a new lustre brightens their eyes. Like King Harry's men before Harfleur, they stand like greyhounds in the slips, straining upon the start.[13]

Right out of the gate, Ervin asserted that the Constitution answers the question, saying:

> There is not a syllable in it which gives the Supreme Court any discretionary power to fashion policies based on such considerations as expediency or prudence to guide the course of action of the government of our country. On the contrary, the Constitution provides in plain and positive terms that the role of the Supreme Court is that of an adjudicator, which determines judicially legal controversies between adverse litigants.
>
> In assigning this role to the Supreme Court, the Founding Fathers were faithful to the dream which inspired them to draft and ratify the Constitution, and to their action in rejecting in the Constitutional Convention repeated proposals that the Supreme Court should act as a council of revision, possess

discretionary power to veto all acts of Congress the justices deemed unwise, no matter how much those acts harmonized with the Constitution.[14]

Ervin insisted that the Founders had studied history; that they knew of the eternal struggle of mankind to throw off the manacles of tyranny and assert the right to govern themselves. They knew also, that all people have an innate desire for power, just as they have a need to pursue their own happiness, and that when President George Washington spoke of "the love of power, and proneness to abuse it" he was articulating an axiom of politics that the powers of public officers must be plainly stated and carefully observed.

Ervin attacked the idea of a court acting as policy maker in a direct way:

> A policy is a definite or settled course of action adopted and followed by government. The power to make policy is discretionary in nature. It involves the making of choices on the basis of expediency or prudence among alternative ways of acting.
>
> The power to make policy in a government of laws resides with those who are authorized to participate in the lawmaking process.
>
> The Founding fathers made policy when they ordained and established the Constitution, which determines the fundamental policies of our country. Since Article I of the Constitution grants Congress the power to make laws and requires every bill passed by it to be presented to the President for his approval or disapproval before it takes effect, the Congress and the President have policymaking power. Moreover, Article V confers upon Congress and the states, acting in conjunction, limited policymaking power, i.e., the power to amend the Constitution.[15]

Having spelled out exactly where the policymaking authority is placed by the constitution, Ervin goes on to specify how and why the Constitution affirmatively denies policymaking power to the Supreme Court.

> Article III denies the Supreme Court policymaking power in plain and positive terms. It does this by making the Supreme Court a court of law and equity and by granting to it "judicial power" only. Under this Article, the Supreme Court has no power whatever except the power to hear and determine cases between adverse litigants, which are within the scope of its original or appellate jurisdiction.
>
> Article III denies the Supreme Court policymaking power in another way. When it is read in conjunction with the supremacy clause of Article VI, Article III obligates Supreme Court Justices to base their decisions in the cases they hear upon the Constitution, the laws, and the treaties of the United States, and thus forbids them to take their personal notions as to what is desirable into account in making their rulings.[16]

When it came his time to speak, Ramsey Clark took a different tack. He made no effort to justify the conclusion that the fourteenth amendment intended to enshrine an unwritten right of privacy, or any other rights not specifically mentioned in the text of the Constitution. Instead, he focused on the problems and challenges of the present and future. Here is a sample:

> Perhaps the major question of our times is whether institutions can change to cope with the vast dynamics of mass urban population and burgeoning technology. The answer is far from clear. Can government be responsive to the needs of its people? Will technology master man? Can violence as an international and interpersonal problem solver be conditioned from human capability? Can we assure human dignity? Will racism divide people who must live together with dignity, respect and love?[17]

Asserting that the challenge of tomorrow requires giving priority to what he calls "the science of effective change," Clark continues with a pragmatic assertion:

> The United States Supreme Court, inherently the most conservative institution within our system of government, has addressed itself to the present and future more effectively than any other agent of our society. Somehow, in these last twenty years, it has detected the greatest needs of our times in the cases that have found their way to its forum and has acted to meet those needs.[18]

Clark then proceeds to chronicle the various cases in which an activist Supreme Court has addressed "the crushing problems of the people." He cites *Baker v. Carr*, 369 U.S. 186 (1962) claiming it liberated government from the nineteenth century. In fact the "one man one vote" case has failed to equalize the representation in the United States Congress, where due to the failure to enact proportional representation as directed by the constitution, there continue to be congressional districts that vary by as much as 100 percent.

He goes on to cite *Brown v. Board of Education* as a stellar example of the Supreme Court's bootstrap solution to racism, then admits that in the sixteen years since the Brown decision, at that time, less than 5 percent of the black children attending school in the South were in racially diverse schools, and he insists that forced busing of children away from their familiar home neighborhoods is required by the United States Constitution.

He complains that the rights created by the Supreme Court in the Miranda and Escobedo cases have not been fully enforced, which casts some doubt even on their justification as practical and necessary regulations, without regard for the Constitutional authority to issue them.

His justification for policymaking by the court, very simply, is need. In these troubled times, Mr. Clark is saying, we need a benign dictator; an oracle which has the power, the mission and the courage to address the challenges of modern society, quickly, directly, and efficiently. Here is how he says it:

> Midst such sweeping change, such vast turbulence, can we hope for mere words—antique phrases—a Constitution, a Bill of Rights—to preserve liberty? Words are not self-executing—even if their meaning is clear.[19]

He then quotes Thoreau:

> If a man does not keep pace with his companion perhaps it is because he hears a different drummer . . . let him step to the music which he hears however measured or far away.[20]

Finally, Ramsey Clark finishes with a peroration calculated to inspire a rousing huzzah from the caring masses:

> Will the immensity of our problems: population, world peace, nuclear armaments, rising crime, racial strife, the decaying hearts of our great central cities, pollution, the sheer numbers in our environment so strain our understanding that we may confuse the essential liberties protected by the Constitution with the causes of our grief? Will we come to fear the strength of diversity, the virtue of difference? Will we see some nonexistent contest between liberty and security; between the rights of the individual and the protection of society? Can complexity and anxiety cause us to doubt that fulfillment is the flower of freedom, borne by no other tree; that freedom is the child of courage? Could we forget that nothing can so debilitate security as deprivation of liberty?[21]

Clark speaks of "We" without telling us exactly who is expected to speak for "us." Thus he asserts that we can both enlarge the rights of the individual and better protect our society, and do it simultaneously. "We" he says, "have the capability." "We need only the will."

It is not, he says, the words of the Constitution that guarantee our liberty, but words that abide in our hearts and minds.

I cannot read the words of Ramsey Clark without harkening back to the law review article I wrote in 1982, "Return to Philadelphia: A Case for the Calling of an Amendatory Convention Under Article V of the Federal Constitution."

At one point, I stated:

> After all, the convention is its best argument. The fact that a convention is, by definition, an exercise of pubic sovereignty makes it intrinsically a desirable thing. The fact that a convention is a solemn deliberative body, concerned—at the constitutional level—at the structural level—with all of the vital issues of today, and the critical concerns of tomorrow makes it per se useful and worthy of support. The fact that a convention is an extraordinary agency, established

> to take the long view of public affairs should attract to its benches the most able of our citizens. No one should doubt that as the United States of America looks to a future endangered by nuclear war, shocked by international terrorism, worried by limited resources, amazed by exploding technology, baffled by moral dilemmas, and still agonized by human suffering, the counsel and the service of the best people are needed.[22]

Both Mr. Clark and I see and agree upon a great many challenges in the future, that need to be addressed by "We" the people. The difference is in our response to those challenges. Clark would have us ignore the supreme law of the land. Indeed, he would have us ignore all written laws, as long as we are steeped in the tradition of the principles of the Constitution that are, wordlessly, to have a treasured place in our minds and hearts. He would install the nine life-appointed Justices of the Supreme Court as the first and final arbiters of life in modern society. My solution was, and is, an Article V convention and a government of laws, not of men.

A NON-PARTISAN COURT

It is safe to say that almost no one in America wants the Supreme Court of the United States to be a partisan institution. Members of Congress, Presidents, the national media, both major political parties, and civic organizations of every stripe gladly pay lip service to the ideal of a Supreme Court that is independent of party loyalties and deaf to pleas for partisan preference.

All of which is not to say that people generally are willing to forgo the possibility of seating Justices who share their particular beliefs. Impanelling a truly non-partisan court will not be accomplished overnight, nor should it. The role of the Court as constitutional interpreter is too vital in our nation to admit of a sudden or sweeping overhaul, such as was proposed by Franklin D. Roosevelt in 1937. A constitutional convention is the right place to discuss what can be done to improve the Supreme Court. While I have repeatedly stated on these pages that a convention sets its own agenda and that I have no thought of dictating anything to the convention, it is none the less true that I have given this matter some thought, and I will take the liberty of sharing here a proposal first advanced by Senator Sam Ervin forty years ago.

Let's start with what is wrong with the court today.

The President has absolute and unlimited power to make appointments to the court. This fact alone assures that the Supreme Court will necessarily be involved in politics. Presidential candidates will promise or infer that they will appoint justices of a particular disposition in an effort to win votes. Thus, there is always a partisan litmus test whenever an appointment is to be made, and appointees of Presidents are expected to reflect the political philosophy of the appointing authority. When they don't, as in the case of Earl Warren, it is news.

A second bad result of unfettered Presidential appointments is the tendency of senior judges to delay retirement pending the election of a President who will replace them with a justice who shares their views. Justices cannot name their successors, but they can wait until they have a sympathetic ear in the White House. The result of this factor, of course, is that superannuated judges stay beyond their productive years.

As we have already seen there is an Ivy Corridor down which a troubling majority of Supreme Court Justices trod under the present regime. The fact is that every state in the Union has, in one way or another, attempted to insulate its judiciary from the vicissitudes of partisan politics. Sam Ervin's proposal taps into the vast resources of the fifty states to provide the manpower needed on the high court.

His plan also eliminates the monstrously political and unseemly circus of Senate confirmation of Supreme Court candidates. Partisan Senators, playing up to their political bases and the news media, not only embarrass the nominees, but also demean the dignity of the office to which they have been nominated. Under the proposal as I present it here, the Chief Justices of the fifty states will have the duty to vet Supreme Court candidates. There will be no need for the Senate to inquire into their qualifications.

The plan does not disrupt the Court. Incumbent Justices are retained. Only their successors are affected by the changes, which include an eighteen year term. Finally, a second paragraph is proposed, which addresses the perennial issue of original intent and the role of the court as an adjudicator.

In summary, the Non-Partisan Court Plan is a gradual changing of the orientation of the Supreme Court. Justices will always be Washington-centered and focused. That is the nature of the beast. They live there, they work there. Their agenda has to do with the Constitution and laws of the nation. But it is fondly to be hoped that the fifty state Chief Justices will nominate men and women who won't forget where they came from.

THE NON-PARTISAN SUPREME COURT PLAN

SECTION ONE: The Supreme Court of the United States of America shall consist of the current nine Justices and their successors, who shall be appointed by the President, without Senate confirmation, for eighteen year terms, from a list of five nominees presented by the Chief Justices of the several States.

SECTION TWO: The Court shall interpret the Constitution and its amendments as understood by the people who ratified them, and it shall render no opinion enlarging or diminishing the powers of the government or the rights of the people.

NOTES

1. Alexander Hamilton, Federalist #1.
2. James Madison, Federalist #53.
3. George Washington, Farewell Address.
4. Alpheus Thomas Mason and William M. Beaney, *The Supreme Court in a Free Society* (New York: W.W. Norton and Company, 1968).
5. Ibid.
6. Thomas McIntyre Cooley, *A Treatise on the Constitutional Limitations*, 1868, reprint 1972.
7. http://www.plannedparenthood.org/ppsne/our-history-20162.htm.
8. *Poe v. Ullman*, 367 U.S. 497 (1961).
9. U.S. Constitution, Amendment #14.
10. U.S. Constitution, Article VII.
11. *New York Times*, "Letter to the Editor," March 9, 1861.
12. Daniel Webster, 1782–1817.
13. Sam Ervin, Jr. and Ramsey Clark, *Role of the Supreme Court: Policy Maker or Adjudicator?* (Washington, DC: American Enterprise Institute, 1970), foreword.
14. Ibid., p. 1.
15. Ibid., p. 5.
16. Ibid., p. 6.
17. Ibid., p. 26.
18. Ibid., p. 27.
19. Ibid., p. 29.
20. Ibid., p. 30.
21. Ibid., p. 30.
22. www.returntophiladelphia.com.

III

The Solution

Chapter Eight

Federalism

The Hamiltonians knew the importance of being in touch with the sentiment of the people. They knew that leadership requires the ability to present new ideas in a positive, acceptable, easily understood format. Labels are critical in the political process, not so much because they give a real definition, but because their connotations will determine whether people will get close enough to a movement, and study it long enough, to understand what it is all about.

Hamilton and his confreres chose the label "Federalists." They could have called themselves Nationalists or Unionists. Such labels certainly would have described more accurately what it was that Hamilton and Madison were trying to do. They saw the need for a strong, national sovereignty.

George Washington, whose valiant efforts on the revolutionary battlefields had won the fledgling nation its freedom, was almost despairing of achieving permanent peace and prosperity. His letters during the period of the Articles of Confederation reveal the bleak outlook that fostered the drive for nationalism among the most prudent leaders of that day. But although prudent, far thinking men in the 1780s realized the need for a stronger national government, practical political considerations and a sensitivity to the feelings, fears and predilections of the public made it necessary to advance the cause of union under a label which reassured those who associated a strong central government with the tyranny of George III.

And so the Hamiltonians chose the word Federalist, to emphasize that their concept of union was one in which the states were inviolable components. Still, they wanted a federal union. It was a national federal government, rather than a mere league of independent states, that they incorporated in the Constitution of 1787. They made it acceptable to the American people, and established and consolidated it so successfully over the next ten years that, when the Jeffersonian era came about and the Federalists passed quietly from the political stage, the principle they had advanced had become an axiom of American government.

It was clever of them to call themselves Federalists. Their opposition, the Patrick Henrys and the stalwarts of state sovereignty, put up an awful hue and cry. Their complaint was that the constitution did not create a federation, but instead created a national government.

Here was Patrick Henry's declamation:

> Have they said, we, the States? Have they made a proposal of a compact between states? If they had, this would be a confederation: It is otherwise most clearly a consolidated government. The question turns, Sir, on that poor little thing-the expression, We, the people, instead of the States, of America. I need not take much pains to show that the principles of this system are extremely pernicious, impolitic, and dangerous. Is this a monarchy, like England; a compact between prince and people, with checks on the former to secure the liberty of the latter? Is this a Confederacy, like Holland; an association of a number of independent states, each of which retains its individual sovereignty? It is not a democracy, wherein the people retain all their rights securely. Had these principles been adhered to, we should not have been brought to this alarming transition, from a Confederacy to a consolidated Government. [1]

In effect, Henry was arguing that the name "Federalist" had been stolen from them. To Patrick Henry, a Federalist would be someone favoring a confederation, and not an advocate of a sovereign national government. His concern is certainly understandable. The idea of dual sovereignty was completely new, completely without precedent in the history books.

Hamilton, Madison, and the others who favored a strong national government, indeed a sovereign national government, preempted the name Federalists as a means of reassuring the people that the states would retain their sovereignty under the new constitution. Fortunately for the country, though unhappily for them, Patrick Henry and his colleagues lost the battle of the slogans. Federalism became the accepted euphemism for nationalism, and the out-maneuvered state supremacists found themselves stuck with the unflattering, negative label of Anti-Federalists.

Half the battle in politics, really, is to get your opponent identified as anti-something. Then you have him in an unattractive, negative, defensive posture. Anti-movements are like sniper's nests or guerrilla warfare. They are effective for harassment and disruption, but they do not, of themselves, support responsible governing coalitions, as the Anti-Federalists of two hundred years ago finally learned. When the Anti-Federalists were able to shake off the negative label and become known as Democratic Republicans, they were able to come to power.

The ancient title "Federalist" is a label that is sufficiently ambiguous to convey a sense of balance. It has a good, sensible, non-radical ring to it. How can a Federalist be a bad guy, when Hamilton, Madison, Washington and John Marshall were all Federalists? How can a Federalist be bent on the destruction of the nation, when federalism carries the historical connotation of nationalism and union? It's a safe word. And yet it is a word full of meaning and pregnant with possibilities for political reform in our times.

Because federalism continues to embrace the opposing notions of national sovereignty and state sovereignty, it continues to express, in a single, agreeable word, the traditional concept of dual sovereignty in the United States. Federalism says that the national government is supreme in its proper sphere, and that the states are supreme in their proper sphere. Two hundred years ago, the first half of that axiom needed assertion and defense. Today, it is the second half of the statement that requires bolstering.

Federalism is still federalism. But the new Federalist differs from the old, not in what he or she stands for, but in the backdrop against which they stand. Surrounded by a clamoring band of state house loyalists, the Federalist of 1788 appeared to be a radical nationalist. In the Washington-dominated economy of 2014, the Federalist is viewed as an anachronistic exponent of states' rights. The very notion of dual sovereignty needs to be re-expressed and re-learned. I fear that sloppy thinking, which has pervaded our elementary and secondary schools for so long, has taken over the rhetoric in colleges, universities, and in the media to such an extent that not even lip service is given any more to the federalist plan of dual sovereignty.

Thirty years ago Ronald Reagan announced a plan called New Federalism, the gist of which was that the national government proposed to transfer responsibility for a number of programs to the governments of the several states. I had to ask myself, "Where is it written that the federal government decides what programs the states are to undertake?"

I reviewed my dog-eared copy of the United States Constitution again and again, but I found nothing. Nowhere does it say that the federal Congress divides the powers and duties of government between itself and the states. Still, if we were to cross examine the average high school civics teacher, we would discover that the common, reasonably well-informed opinion in America makes no distinction between the relationship of the states to the national government and the relationship of the counties and cities to the states.

Particularly since the advent of local home rule in the cities and counties, the principle of local autonomy is generally accepted. As a matter of political theory, it is widely believed that a governmental function is best, most efficiently performed, if it is at all possible, by the unit of government that is closest to the people.

By definition, government is the permission of the people to use force against those who break the law. People have more confidence in the benign use of force that is closer to home. A neighbor with a gun is less threatening than a stranger with a gun. Local control and local accountability—home rule—keeps the coercive power of government closer to home.

There is, of course, a difference between home rule and dual sovereignty. City or county home rule is the creation of the state. Cities and counties are the creatures of the state. State statutes and state constitutions can abolish or alter local municipalities, change their boundaries, their powers or their status. Municipalities are subdivisions of state government, wholly subservient to the states and wholly dependent upon the states for their continued existence and authority.

And so it is entirely within the province of state government to impose duties upon counties and cities, and to declare which functions will be performed at the state level and which at the local level. It is all a matter of organization, and the only principle involved, constitutionally speaking, is that of equal protection of the laws as it relates to the evenhanded treatment of various classes of municipalities by the general government of the state.

The relationship of the states to the federal government is different. The states are not subdivisions of the national government. The states are sovereign components of the federal union. The states are, with respect to their proper sphere of authority, as final and independent as the government of the United States. The powers of the state governments are not traceable to the federal government. Their powers are traceable to their respective constitutions adopted by their indigenous people.

THE ECONOMY

Now, this dry, and I fear uninspiring, discourse on the theory of dual sovereignty is not without some importance in our day. Indeed, the proper role of the states in our scheme of representative democracy is a particularly timely subject as we struggle with a sputtering economy. In that connection, I want to make two general observations before proposing some solutions.

First, it seems to me that the phenomena of recession and depression are not so much national ones as we have been led to believe. I remember seeing a news story some years ago reporting that twenty-one of the American states were experiencing double-digit unemployment. The existence of double-digit unemployment is no surprise to me. I am from Michigan. In Michigan we talk about cities with 16 or 17 percent unemployment as being pockets of prosperity.

What did interest me about the story is that there must be twenty-nine states that do not have double-digit unemployment. The suggestion is that some of them may be doing relatively well, that there are good times in the South and the West, just as there are hard times in the East and the North.

In the decennial census of 2010 it appeared that, were it not for the extension of life expectancy, the industrial states of the Northeast and the Midwest would have experienced actual population declines in the first decade of the twenty-first century. In the East more people are moving out than are moving in. Here are some interesting numbers: In the ten years from 2000 to 2010, the population of Nevada increased by 35.1 percent; the population of Arizona increased by 24.6 percent; the population of Utah increased by 23.8 percent; the population of Idaho increased by 21.1 percent; and the population of Texas increased by 20.6 percent.

In that same decade, the population of New York increased by 2.1 percent; the population of Ohio increased by 1.6 percent; the population of Louisiana increased by 1.4 percent; the population of Rhode Island increased by only four-tenths of 1 percent; and the population of the great and sovereign state of Michigan *decreased* by six-tenths of 1 percent. In my home state of Michigan you see losses of jobs, plant closings, school closings, and an exodus of people and investment capital.

I do not present these matters as a mere litany of woes, but to demonstrate what I believe is an important principle of economics, which needs to be considered now. People live and work and raise their families in the states. They build their churches and schools in the states. They die and are buried in the states. For most of us, the economy of our state is a good deal more important in our daily lives than is the economy of the nation.

The national economy is a blur of numbers printed in The Wall Street Journal, a staccato of statistics punctuating the nightly news. The state and local economy is seen and understood in terms of busy or empty stores, friends and relatives working or out of work, savings accumulating or being used up. We have the Farm Belt, the Sun Belt, and the Snow Belt; manufacturing states, recreational states, and financial centers; populations that are predominantly young or old, skilled or unskilled, urban or rural; we are not a homogeneous nation, but a composite of local, state and regional interests and concerns.

There is not a single American economy, but fifty different state economies. These are more or less grouped by regions, but even within the regions there are important variations, because different people have made different choices, because they have dealt with similar problems in different ways from state to state. This is my first point: the states are not merely historical units of government, but separate economic entities, whose prosperity is only partially affected by national trends and policies.

The second point is closely related to the first, and it is simply this: the federal government is incompetent to manage the economy of the whole nation. I would like to support that assertion with three observations. First, the federal Constitution did not design a national government for the purpose of managing the economy. Our forefathers had more limited, classical governmental functions in mind. The form of government they devised was suited to making political choices, but not for making business judgments.

In addition, the economy is too diverse to be controlled from a single nerve-center and too varied to respond to uniform national solutions. Third, and finally, I submit as evidence of the federal government's incompetence to manage the national economy the dismal failure of so many well-intentioned public servants to assure us of prosperity, to pay our bills, to repay our national obligations.

When this essay was first written thirty years ago, I talked about a national debt which then exceeded $1 trillion; a generation of deficit spending, with annual deficits soon to top the $100 billion mark; the inability to keep promises to, and meet the expectations of, senior citizens, students, the sick, the poor, the disabled, minorities, veterans, refugees, and all the other segments of our population who had come to rely upon entitlements; the inability of our nation to keep abreast of the military capability of adversaries and potential adversaries around the world; all of these danger signs, coming as they did in spite of the best efforts of Ronald Reagan, a President committed to fiscal responsibility and holding an impressive popular mandate for reordering the national establishment.

All of which pointed, I said in 1982, to one incontrovertible, uncomfortable, and unavoidable fact: that our problems are not temporary or political, that our difficulties cannot be ascribed to one political party or the other, or attributed to a few officeholders or to a particular policy, but that our problems are structural. They relate to the balance of power within the federal government and between the federal government and the states.

Today, we have a different political party in power, but the facts are the same and the numbers are incrementally higher: annual deficits of three trillion and a national debt of seventeen trillion. Nothing has happened to refute the conclusion that our problems are structural.

THE LAST PREROGATIVE

It would seem apparent to any thinking person that structural problems do not respond to superficial solutions. You can't cure lung cancer with cough drops. We need to make some major changes. No one listened in the 1980s. The American people must start listening now. The tap, tap, tap of Uncle Sam, buried in the collapsed mine of short-term fixes must awaken the spirit of first responders all across the land. This must become the decade of constitutional reform in the United States. If we are to secure the blessings of liberty to ourselves and to future generations, in the third century of our independence, we, the people, must fix the government. The people created the government; only the people can fix it.

The impetus for that reform will not come from the national government in Washington. It will not come from the state governments. The reform movement has already begun. It is not led or populated by elected officials, either state or federal. It is led by citizens. Ordinary citizens. Interested citizens. First Responders, if you will, who realize that something must be done and that the people currently holding public office at every level simply do not have the will to act.

Article V of the federal Constitution establishes the minimum level of participation in an amendatory constitutional convention. Two-thirds of the states must be represented. The people of two-thirds of the states must come together in order for a convention to exist. A convention is a constituent assembly. Obviously, the whole population of a state cannot attend or participate in a convention. The people must be represented.

Spontaneous grassroots organizations like the Tea Parties or the Occupy movement, typically develop local components in various parts of the nation. But they work together only sporadically. They do not have a game plan. They are all about education, communication, and tying to move the mountain of existing governmental structures.

An Article V convention organized by the citizenry needs volunteers, but they cannot be mere random participants. To have credibility and legitimacy, the delegates must represent the entire nation and they must assert a claim of legitimacy in every community.

Convention USA provides the structure by which it can be done. The 50K apportionment plan, from which 6,166 delegates are to be chosen can be seen on the Internet at www.conventionusa.org.

The mechanics of conducting local elections on the Internet can be rolled out in a matter of months. All it takes is a lot of people and a little money.

Admittedly, what is proposed here is revolutionary. But it is not a rebellion. It does not aim to oust or overthrow the government. Quite the contrary, its goal is to initiate the very remedy provided by the founders of our nation in the 1787 constitution. No one here is talking about a march or a sit-in. No one here is advocating confrontation or protest. No one looks to incumbent officeholders for redress of their grievances.

This effort is self help of the purest and most honorable kind. What is needed in America today is statesmanship. What is needed is thoughtful, open-minded deliberation.

The right to conduct an amendatory convention under Article V of the federal Constitution is the last prerogative of the people of the several sovereign states of the American union. If dual sovereignty means anything in the United States anymore, if there is any irreducible minimum beyond which the lawful authority and inherent power of the states cannot be diminished, it must lie in the clear mandate of Article V. By the plain words of Article V, the people of three-fourths of the states can amend the Constitution of the nation. Speaking either through their state legislatures or through state ratification conventions, the people of the fifty states, counted state by state, are the ultimate sovereign authority by which the federal Constitution is amended.

But the right and the reserved power of the people of the states to pass upon constitutional amendments is hollow indeed without the prerogative of actually conducting an amendatory convention to discuss, refine, draft and propose amendments.

There is no danger of a runaway convention. That phrase, "runaway convention," and all the accompanying horror stories about repealing the Bill of Rights are utterly without substance. They are myths, harmful to democracy, invented by those who are afraid to let the people exercise their historic and God-given right to self-government. Of course, that phrase "runaway convention" is a deliciously effective political slogan. It conjures up all kinds of mental images, mostly of wild, madcap sessions of the political conventions at which the national Democratic and Republican Parties nominate candidates for President and Vice-President. Who wants to let the Constitution of the United States be amended by a bunch of screaming, chanting, flag-waving, sign-carrying, people wearing funny hats and tooting toy horns?

That picture, of course, is totally inapplicable to a solemn, deliberative, national constitutional convention. We are not talking about an exhibition of political enthusiasm that is repeated every four years as the kickoff for a presidential campaign. We are talking about a significant exercise of statesmanship that has not occurred for two hundred years and which will affect the lives and fortunes of millions of human beings long after every person alive today has passed from the earth.

Because the convention is a solemn and significant undertaking, there are those who seek to forestall it by the technique of spraying the issue with question marks. They insist that the convention is new and untried. No one knows how it would work. There are unanswered questions. How are the delegates to be selected? Where would it meet? Who pays for it? Who is eligible to be a delegate? And on and on. Some people want Congress to legislate ground rules for the convention, as though the exercise of fundamental political sovereignty can somehow be codified and neatly contained in rules. All this question-raising and head-scratching and chin-stroking is irrelevant and unnecessary. Article V is nothing if not a self-executing acknowledgment of the sovereignty of the people of the several states in relation to constitution-making and constitutional amendments.

For nearly two hundred years, the state legislatures have been applying for conventions pursuant to Article V. They have not needed congressional permission to do so, nor have they awaited congressional guidelines before invoking their constitutional power to apply for a convention. All the procedural questions can be answered by reference to the words of Article V, the nature of the convention and the historical precedent of the constitutional convention in Philadelphia in 1787. There is no need for any new rules to guide the convention. The convention can organize itself, and perform its historic function just as its predecessors at both the state and national levels have done.

MONEY, MONEY

One subject that surely should be on the convention's agenda is the matter of fiscal responsibility. The inability of the federal establishment to act responsibly with respect to the nation's finances is the shame and disgrace of every generation of Americans in the last one hundred years. Only a constitutional convention can right the ship of state. This fact was brought home forcefully when a drive to hold an Article V convention to propose a balanced budget amendment was side tracked by the Gramm-Rudman-Hollings Act, an exercise in legislative smoke and mirrors which didn't balance the budget and didn't stay on the statute books for vey long, either. Proof that the congressional fox is a very poor guardian of the constitutional hen house, that act was a an illusion designed to derail a burgeoning drive for an Article V convention.

The wording of the Gramm-Rudmand-Hollings Act would not have surprised Madison, Hamilton, and Jay, the authors of the Federalist Papers. They understood human nature. They knew that whenever it is possible to use the wealth of a nation to purchase political popularity for elected officeholders, to corrupt the power of taxation and abuse the public credit as a means of keeping incumbent officeholders in power, the weakness and cupidity of human nature will conspire to assure that common resources will be wasted and the labor of future generations given over to the bondage of public debt.

George Washington warned us that the preservation of public credit is the first measure of national defense. He urged us to pay off, during times of peace, those debts made necessary by war, so as not to cast, ungenerously, upon our children the obligations which we ought to bear ourselves.

Despite the befuddlement of some modern economists, government fiscal responsibility is not, as sometimes urged, a mere question of transient political or economic policy, better left to statutory or administrative regulation than constitutional mandate. The Congress is already empowered by the Constitution to lay and collect taxes for the purpose of paying the debts of the United States. I seriously doubt that any of the delegates who labored through that hot summer of 1787 to write the Constitution would have believed for a moment that Congress might someday neglect or refuse to lay and collect taxes to pay the debts of the United States and persist in that refusal year in and year out until more than $17 trillion of unpaid obligations had accumulated.

Indeed, I think that any fair reading of Article I, Section 8 of the Constitution would yield the conclusion that if the common defense and the general welfare are things that ought to be provided for, debts of the United States are things that ought to be paid.

Fiscal responsibility is not a matter of politics or economic policy. Capitalist states can be run on red ink, and socialist regimes can have balanced budgets. Fiscal responsibility is not merely the platform of a political party or the goal of a particular administration. It is a measure of the credibility and viability of the established institution of government itself.

Nor is fiscal responsibility a matter of choice. The effects of fiscal irresponsibility are not immediate, but they are certain. We know that our government is deeply committed as the guarantor of the nation's economy. The government stands behind mortgage loans, business loans, and student loans. The government protects our bank deposits and bond issues. These secondary obligations are so immense that they dwarf even the monstrous primary public debt, not to mention the moral commitment that underlies our many national entitlement programs.

If we default on these obligations, we can expect nothing less than civil disorder. This is an irrefutable lesson of history. Shay's Rebellion, the Whiskey Rebellion, the Veteran's March, and the Welfare Marches show that the American people are not apathetic when they are hungry or homeless. They will not exchange a lifetime of savings for a fistful of worthless script without a fight. In such an extreme case, the American people will show no more restraint in preserving the institutions of government than they will be inclined to protect the unhappy temporary occupants of public office.

In summary, I submit the following propositions. Since fiscal integrity relates to the stability of our system of government, the means of assuring it belong in our Constitution. The proper constitutional means of assuring the fiscal responsibility and integrity of the union can only be reliably proposed by a body of citizens which is not itself participating in the excesses to be guarded against. An amendatory convention called pursuant to Article V of the United States Constitution is such a body, created and intended by our forefathers precisely for the purpose of enabling the sovereign people of the several states of the American union, without bloodshed, to assert their last prerogative as free men and women: to alter the form of the government (as it was said in the declaration of independence), "laying its foundation on such principles and organizing its powers in such form, as to them shall seem most likely to effect their safety and happiness."

Finally, I submit that the act of convening an amendatory convention under Article V would in itself be more significant than whatever particular amendment or amendments might be agreed upon as a result of it. The convention itself represents a return to first principles. It represents a reassertion of the right of self-determination, and a return to representative democracy in America. I can think of no cause more worthy of any responsible citizen's best efforts and total commitment.

The Convention contemplated by Article V need not be a short-lived or temporary effort. Quite the opposite. We have waited too long, tolerated government by a professional political oligarchy for too many years, to expect that we can right the ship of state with a single turn of the rudder.

The convention should, the convention must, be a permanent establishment, standing at the ready to plug whatever loopholes the ingenuity of self-serving politicians should invent or discover in the bulwarks of our national republic.

There are many Americans who believe that what must be done immediately is the adoption of a balanced budget amendment. Others propose that state legislatures be given the power to veto Congressional enactments, especially Congressional bills raising the "debt ceiling." As desirable as a balanced budget amendment may be, none of those amendments which have circulated around the country are a complete or final solution to the mindless irresponsibility that has been building a house of cards in the nation's capital for the last half century.

Just trying to require balanced budgets without paring down the nationwide scope of federal domestic expenditures is doomed to failure and frustration. The massive national debt is not simply a matter of overspending on the proper objects of federal expenditure. It is the consequence of a drift toward accumulating all domestic sovereignty under the dome of the national Capital.

The horse-trading and pork-barreling of the career politicians who direct federal money to their home states has the cumulative effect of undermining state-based efforts to solve local problems using local resources. Much of that problem can be attributed to the sixteenth amendment.

Adopted in 1913, the sixteenth amendment gave the national government the authority to levy taxes on incomes without apportionment by states, as required by Section 2 of Article I of the 1787 Constitution. It was the dawn of big government in the United States. Today, one hundred years later, income taxes, in the form of payroll taxes and both corporate and individual income taxes amount to 91 percent of the revenue of the national government.

In an era when the federal government spends $3 trillion a year more than it takes in, adding that deficit to a national debt that swells by a million dollars every seventy-five seconds, it can be fairly assumed that the federal income tax rates are as high as the dynamics of political activity will permit. In short, Uncle Sam takes as much of the taxpayers' money as the ballot box will allow.

Essentially, this leaves nothing for the states. If the federal government sucks up all the available income tax, there is nothing left for the states. Their only recourse is to troop to Washington hat in hand and beg for a rebate of some of the money they have sent to the national government.

Unfortunately, all federal money comes with federal regulation, and bit by bit, the sovereignty of the several states is purchased by the national government. The golden rule: "He who has the gold makes the rules" dictates that local decision making is transferred to Washington, DC with every dollar a Congressman or Senator finagles for his or her constituents.

Several state legislatures have passed Article V resolutions in hopes of triggering a convention to propose a revenue sharing amendment. At the root of this initiative is another barnacle on the ship of state. Federal bureaucracies, enflamed with zeal to manage the local affairs of the states, while being unable to convince Congress to fully fund their programs, nonetheless issue regulations, the failure to observe which will trigger the loss of whatever federal financial assistance there may be.

All of which results in federal encroachment on state sovereignty. With a sometimes minimal contribution to the cost of a program, the federal government "buys" control of the program. Over time, the financial consequences that enabled the federal government to make the rules are forgotten, and all that remains are the dictates of the national bureaucracy and the near universal presumption that federal authority trumps that of the states.

The relation between national and state level taxing authority is a subject that clearly belongs on the agenda of an amendatory constitutional convention. Here is one possible approach:

> The Sixteenth Amendment is hereby amended by the addition of the following words: Taxes laid and collected by the several states on the income taxed on the authority of this Amendment shall be a credit against one half of such federal taxes.

Dividing the people's hard-earned tax dollars equally between state and federal treasuries will make the concept of dual sovereignty a reality. It will, of course, substantially reduce the national government's income, but since it will increase state revenues, it should enable the states to underwrite those activities that belong in their portfolios, while incentivizing the national government to discontinue encroaching on state sovereignty.

DECAPITATING WASHINGTON

Article I, Section 8, Paragraph 17 of the Constitution of the United States says that the Congress shall have the power:

> To exercise exclusive Legislation in all Cases whatsoever over such District (not to exceed ten miles square) as may, by Cession of particular States and the acceptance of Congress become the Seat of the Government of the United States

Virginia donated thirty-nine square miles and Maryland contributed the other sixty-one square miles. And so the District of Columbia was born. In 1791, it was named the City of Washington, in honor of the first President.

In 1801, the so-called Organic Act, organized the District into two counties and officially ended the Maryland and Virginia state citizenship of the inhabitants.

In 1846, the folks on the Virginia side of the Potomac persuaded their legislature and the Congress to undo the deal they made in 1790, and give the thirty-nine square miles back to the Commonwealth. All that was left of the District of Columbia was the sixty-one square miles donated by Maryland.

The Twenty-Third Amendment to the U.S. Constitution ratified in 1961 gives the residents of the District of Columbia the right to vote for President of the United States. It gave the District three votes in the Electoral College, equal to the smallest of the fifty states.

By Act of Congress, the people of Washington are allowed two non-voting members of the House of Representatives. The citizens in the District have no voice in the Senate.

In 1978, Congress passed and sent to the states a proposed constitutional amendment that would have given the District senators and congressmen equal to a state. That amendment failed after getting only nineteen state ratifications in seven years.

The District of Columbia is an unfortunate anomaly in our federal republic. Like a lump in the mattress, the District of Columbia does not fit with the rest of the nation. It is neither a federal territory like Guam or Puerto Rico, nor is it a territory in the sense that Alaska and Hawaii were before becoming states.

There is no groundswell of support to admit the District to the Union as the fifty-first state, although its population is slightly larger than that of Wyoming. Still there is a continuing discomfort with the fact that the citizens of the District do not enjoy the same dual citizenship and domestic sovereignty as the residents of the fifty states.

Moreover, the idea of a Capital City which is no real part of the Union of sovereign states that defines the United States of America is discomfiting.

More than just an historical curiosity, the District's disconnectedness lends an air of special privilege and insider camaraderie that exacerbates the alienation of the states from the nation. The Founders of our nation never intended Americans to be ruled by a coterie of elite managers living in Vaticanesque isolation.

More that 600,000 people live and work inside the beltway. They are the clerks, the staffers, the middle managers, the bureaucrats who run our national government. For them, Uncle Sam is the end all and be all of American political power and authority. Is it any wonder then, that the administrative rules they draft and the bureaucratic decisions they make reflect an attitude that the states are merely administrative departments of the single, omnipotent national authority of the national government?

Increasingly, Americans are reawakening to the importance of state sovereignty in matters of domestic governance. Massive, top-down national social programs like affordable health care that is neither affordable nor desirable health care, are causing Americans to look more and more to their state governments for effective answers.

It seems to me that an important first step in dismantling the ubiquitous national nanny would be to eliminate the isolated island of imperial importance that fosters the aura of omnipotence in our nation's capital.

My suggestion:

> The Twenty-Third Amendment is hereby repealed, and all lands ceded to the United States for the seat of government are returned to the Commonwealth of Virginia and the State of Maryland respectively.

The Pentagon is in Virginia. There is no reason why the White House can't be in Maryland. And no reason why the people of Washington should have no votes in Congress but more to say about who is President than the citizens in forty-nine of the fifty states.

This kind of an amendment is hardly something sufficiently of interest to the fifty state legislatures to induce them to petition for an Article V convention for the sole purpose of proposing it, but it is an example of some constitutional housekeeping that a permanent convention could be expected to address.

Constitutional reform, as we have noted before, is no sport for the short-winded. The lessons learned from two hundred years of governance under our beloved constitution are not always apparent or universally understood. Ongoing, institutional study, discussion, debate, and decision about the constitutional system are the only ways the consent of the governed can be kept current and articulated by every generation.

Thomas Jefferson thought the Constitution should be reconsidered every nineteen years. He also opined that the tree of liberty should be nourished with the blood of tyrants and patriots from time to time as well.

I have no doubt that Mr. Jefferson would applaud an initiative to establish a permanent amendatory constitutional convention after two hundred and thirty years of benign neglect, even if it required a bloodless revolution by 6,166 patriotic First Responders.

DEBTS AND DEFICITS

Section 8 of Article I of the federal Constitution grants to Congress the power to Borrow money on the credit of the United States. The same section also gives Congress the power to coin money, and regulate the value thereof. I have always mused over those two provisions. If Congress has the power to coin money, why would it ever be necessary to borrow money? Most assuredly, if I had a printing press in my basement that produced authentic hundred dollar bills, I would never borrow money. Why then, if the government can coin money, should it ever have to borrow money?

In a November 26, 1798 letter Thomas Jefferson sent to his friend, John Taylor, he observed:

> I wish it were possible to obtain a single amendment to our constitution; I would be willing to depend on that alone for the reduction of the administration of our government to the genuine principles of its constitution. I mean an additional article taking from the federal government the power of borrowing.[2]

Many people support what is called "the gold standard." By that phrase, they mean a currency which has a fixed relationship to the value of gold. When Sir Isaac Newton, the same man who discovered the laws of gravity, was master of the British Mint in 1717, he proclaimed that gold was worth $20 a troy ounce. Perhaps he thought that a fixed value for gold would have the same beneficial effect as the natural pull of gravitation.

He may have been correct. Gold held the value Newton gave it for 217 years until 1934. In 1933, President Roosevelt closed all American banks for three days, then required everyone to deposit their gold in a bank, under threat of fine or imprisonment. Further, Congress outlawed the private possession of gold, except for necessary commercial or artistic uses.

After the Second World War with the Bretton Woods Agreement, the United States agreed to support the value of gold at $35 per ounce, buying any gold offered at that price, and selling off its gold reserves at the same price when the market threatened to rise above $35 per ounce.

In 1971, President Richard Nixon terminated support of gold at $35 per ounce and raised the price to $38. In 1972, after an attempt to support the price at $42.22 per troy ounce, The United States got out of the market and allowed the price of gold to be determined by market forces.

In 1974, during the administration of President Gerald Ford, all sanctions against private ownership and possession of gold were repealed, and gold became truly a commodity. In March of 2014, the market price was 1,353 USD for one troy ounce of gold.

The difficulty with coining money is to find some external basis of value which is safe from manipulation by buyers and sellers. Obviously, a commodity, such as gold, being bought and sold in the market place, cannot be the measure of its own value.

The constitutional power and duty of the American government to "coin money" is essentially an obligation to provide the people with a stable, reliable medium of commercial exchange. Alexander Hamilton wanted a national bank. He got it in 1791, but its twenty-year year charter was not renewed in 1811. A second national bank was created in 1817, but President Andrew Jackson vetoed the renewal of its twenty-year year charter in 1836. In 1863, to help finance the Civil War, Congress created a system of national banks, whose bank notes were backed by U.S. government bonds.

The titular head of the nation's money system is the Comptroller of the Currency, who, despite the sound of that title, does not control the currency. He or she is essentially the head of the banking police who devote their time and energy making sure that the chartered national banks do not violate the laws.

The full faith and credit of the United States stands behind the $17 trillion national debt. The full faith and credit of the United States also stands behind the currency issued by the United States Treasury. There is almost no difference between a hundred dollar bill and a hundred dollar bond, except that the bond carries the obligation to pay interest and one other important thing.

The bond only entitles the holder to be paid in money. Money carries another, vitally important feature: it is legal tender for all debts, public and private. And what, pray tell, is legal tender? Very simply, legal tender is the full force of government, from a summons to a jail cell, from a police officer's pistol to an atom bomb.

This is what is called fiat money. Fiat is simply a Latin word meaning "let it be." American fiat money is money simply because the United States government says it is money. How much money can the government make? That is the ultimate question. If the government can effectively make all the money that our leaders or our people want or ask for, the effort to print ourselves into prosperity will fail. There are dozens of horrible examples of that policy in other countries, as well as a few in our own history.

There just aren't enough bailiffs or jail cells to force people to accept fiat money that has lost its charm. If some people don't want your money, you can make them take it. If nobody wants it, you can't even hire a bill collector.

I submit that common sense dictates that there should be a constitutional standard for the nation's money supply. Unlike the regularly increased Congressional debt ceiling, a constitutional currency standard would effectively discipline the legislature. It would make balanced budgets mandatory.

The subject of fiscal responsibility needs to be on the agenda of an amendatory constitutional convention. To open discussion, I would suggest something like this:

FISCAL RESPONSIBILITY AMENDMENT

SECTION 1: The Congress shall not have the power to borrow money.

SECTION 2: The Congress shall have the power to authorize the issuance of currency, in whatever form, including electronically enabled metal and plastic, up to a total face value of $100,000 multiplied by the population of the United States according to the most recent decennial census.

SECTION 3: Any public official, who, for whatever reason, knowingly emits, authorizes the emission, or conspires to emit more currency than permitted by this Article, shall be guilty of a felony and subject to impeachment.

SECTION 4: In case of a sudden, unanticipated emergency, which shall be described in the Act, the Congress may levy a one-time emergency tax on bank accounts.

An emergency tax may sound draconian, but it has a built in safety valve. If the emergency is not great enough, or severe enough to warrant an emergency tax, then it simply isn't a constitutional emergency. Had a one-time, one percent tax on all bank accounts been proposed to pay for the cost of the 9-11 attack or Hurricane Katrina, it may have been politically feasible, but an emergency tax to avoid an annual deficit would be a very hard sell, even to a Congress given to political pandering.

CLIVEN BUNDY

The real estate that later became the State of Nevada was acquired by the United States by virtue of the Treaty of Guadalupe Hidalgo in 1848, which ended the Mexican War and called for the payment of some $15 million to Mexico by the victorious United States.

Sixteen years later, the Congress of the United States authorized the folks in the Nevada territory, without the usually required 60,000 inhabitants, to hold a constitutional convention and apply for admission to the union.

It was 1864. The Civil War was in full bloom, and Lincoln was running for a second term. The Nevada constitution was adopted on October 31, just eight days before the election and was immediately telegraphed verbatim to Washington, DC. It was the most expensive telegraph ever sent, costing $3,416.77.

And so it was, that on the thirty-first day of October, 1864, President Abraham Lincoln issued a proclamation, declaring Nevada to be admitted to the Union on an equal footing with the original states.

The Constitution of Nevada, which was approved by the President and the Congress of the United States begins with these words: "All political power is inherent in the people."

That statement, common to the constitutions of most of the American states, is not a mere academic observation. Used in a constitution, it is an assertion of sovereignty.

The Nevada constitution contained another provision, required by the Congressional enactment that authorized the drafting of a constitution for the state. It said:

> Third. That the people inhabiting said territory do agree and declare, that they forever disclaim all right and title to the unappropriated public lands lying within said territory, and that the same shall be and remain at the sole and entire disposition of the United States; and that lands belonging to citizens of the United States, residing without the said state, shall never be taxed higher than the land belonging to the residents thereof; and that no taxes shall be imposed by said state on lands or property therein belonging to, or which may hereafter be purchased by, the United States, unless otherwise provided by the Congress of the United States.[3]

This provision is at odds with the declaration that Nevada was admitted to the Union on an equal footing with the original thirteen states. The original thirteen states not only owned all unoccupied land within their borders, they also asserted various claims to the lands between the Appalachian Mountains and the Mississippi River. After adoption of the constitution, the original states ceded all those extra territorial lands to the federal government.

Something like 86 percent of the land mass of the state of Nevada is owned by the federal government. The legal effect of that ownership recently became a matter of public discussion due to the refusal of one Cliven Bundy to pay grazing fees to the federal Bureau of Land Management. Bundy, although not represented by counsel, appears to be claiming that his family has used the public lands adjacent to their ranch since the 1870s, and he therefore has prescriptive rights to continue doing so.

An armed confrontation between the Bureau of Land Management and Bundy's supporters attracted a great deal of public notice, and despite the government's decision to return confiscated Bundy cattle, the legal issue continues to be debated.

It is difficult for most Americans to understand the distinction between ownership and sovereignty. Sovereignty, very simply is the right to use force to impose your will. It is the right to govern. The right to rule. The right to make laws.

Ownership of land, on the other hand, is the right to occupy and to use real estate, in accordance with the laws made by that of the sovereign government.

Here is what the Constitution of the United States says about the federal land: Article I, Section 8 of the United States Constitution provides:

> [Congress shall have the power] To exercise exclusive Legislation in all Cases whatsoever, over such District (not exceeding ten Miles square) as may, by Cession of particular States, and the Acceptance of Congress, become the Seat of the Government of the United States, and to exercise like Authority over all Places purchased by the Consent of the Legislature of the State in which the Same shall be, for the Erection of Forts, Magazines, Arsenals, dock Yards, and other needful Buildings . . .

So, under the Constitution, the federal government's exclusive right to make laws concerning land in the United States, is limited to Washington, DC. and such other land as complies with these four conditions:

1. It has purchased
2. With the consent of the state legislature
3. For forts, magazines, arsenals, dock yards
4. And other needful buildings

Please note that Article I, Section 8 does not mention:

1. parks
2. wet lands
3. habitats for endangered species
4. forests
5. mineral rights
6. grazing rights
7. renting land to others as a source of revenue
8. etc., etc., etc.

No one questions the right of the United States to make laws concerning real estate *outside the United States* (i.e., Guam, Puerto Rico, etc.). But inside the United States, the federal government has no power to make laws concerning real estate, except as granted under Article I, Section 8. And that means it has no power to make laws concerned vacant land situated in one of the fifty States.

So what can the federal government do with 86 percent of Nevada? Just three things:

1. sell it
2. give it to the state or some other entities.
3. use it as an owner, pursuant to the laws of the state in which it is located.

In recent months the Western Governors Association consisting of the governors of seventeen western states and three federal territories, has struggled with the problems of federal land management. Unfortunately, the federal authorities do not recognize the sovereignty of the states in which federally owned lands are located and tend to treat federal lands inside the United States the same as federal lands in territories outside of the borders of any state.

Unlike other nations, sovereignty in the United States is dual; it is divided between the states and the national government. The national government has international sovereignty as a member of the family of nations on the planet. It also has interstate sovereignty, as defined in the United States Constitution, to regulate commerce among the several states of the American union.

The states have domestic sovereignty, which is often called the police power. It is the authority to regulate the affairs of the people. It encompasses the full range of governmental control over the activities of the people; criminal laws, marriage laws, real estate laws, corporations, education, licensing professions, occupations and businesses, health care. The list goes on and on. Basically, the domestic sovereignty of the states includes the right to legislate on any and every subject, unless there is an express constitutional prohibition.

The sovereignty of the national government is just the opposite. The United States may only legislate on subjects specified in the national constitution.

The United States of America owns millions of acres of land in Nevada. But it does not own that land in the same sense that it owns Puerto Rico or Guam. It owns that land in the same sense that it owns post office buildings and federal courthouses all over the country.

It owns that land subject to the domestic sovereignty of the state of Nevada. The United States has no more rights to the land upon which Mr. Bundy has been grazing his cattle than Exxon or General Motors or Bill Gates would have if they owned the land.

If your dog wanders into my yard, I don't own your dog. I can't kill your dog, I can't sell your dog and I can't refuse to give it back to you. If you build a house on my lot, without permission and live there for twenty years, or whatever period of adverse possession is required by state law, you will own the lot. If you build a baseball field on my lot and use it without my permission, for a period defined by state law, you will, by prescription, create an easement that will allow you to continue playing baseball there.

Whatever rights Mr. Bundy has to graze his cattle on federal land should be determined by Nevada courts according to Nevada law. Whatever rights the United States has to keep Bundy from grazing his cattle on federal land should be determined and enforced by Nevada law.

The United States of America may own the land next to Bundy's home, but it is not the domestic sovereign on such lands. It does not have police power there. It can no more shoot people for trespassing than any other land owner in Nevada.

NOTES

1. Patrick Henry, Virginia Ratifying Convention, June 4, 1788.
2. Thomas Jefferson, "Letter to John Taylor," dated November 26, 1798.
3. http://www.leg.state.nv.us/const/nvconst.html

Chapter Nine

The Convention

The history of our nation confirms that the people of the United States have the power and the right to send delegates to a national convention for the purpose of amending the federal Constitution. The record is clear that the impetus for the convention of 1787 came not from the Congress of the Confederation, but from the individual states that answered the call drafted in Annapolis in September of 1786.

The precedent is fully discussed in chapter 2, and the proposal was put forth there that a similar strategy ought to be followed whenever a recalcitrant Congress fails or refuses to call an Article V convention.

Article V specifies that such a convention is to be called upon the request of two-thirds of the states. This is an important threshold. The Founders thought it reasonable to initiate discussion and debate when two-thirds of the states were agreed to do so, even though they required a super majority of three-quarters of the states in order to ratify a proposed constitutional amendment.

The convention of 1787 went forward with its work without the participation of Rhode Island. They assumed that representation from seven states, a bare majority of the original thirteen states, would constitute a quorum. That number was achieved on Friday, May 25, 1787.

It is significant that the Founders did not provide in Article V for the calling of a convention at the request of a bare majority of the states. By requiring the concurrence of two-thirds of the states in order to convene, the Founders obviously intended that two-thirds of the states would be the minimum participation required of an Article V convention.

It follows that when two-thirds of the states want to talk about amending the constitution, they have the constitutional authority to do so. Conversely, whenever an Article V convention is no longer supported by two-thirds of the states, it will have lost the constitutional basis for its legitimacy. In effect, this gives any combination of seventeen states the power to walk out and terminate an Article V convention.

Moreover, if the convention is only attended by a bare two-thirds of the states, every one of them would have a de facto veto, because by leaving, they could prevent the convention from doing business. These inferences should give some measure of comfort to state legislators who fret about a 'run away' convention. As long as they can walk away, they need not fear a "runaway."

Despite these rather obvious considerations, it is safe to say that support for an Article V convention is not overwhelming in the fifty state capitals. In chapter 2 the suggestion is advanced that the states should now consider following the Annapolis precedent and should now invite each other to send delegates to an amendatory convention.

A form of concurrent resolution is offered there. It addresses the troublesome question of how the convention would be organized and how it would vote. Concurrent state by state votes and delegate majority votes are described and labeled the 'convention compromise.'

Certainly there is support among the citizenry for such a process, and no doubt a grassroots showing of support for a state-initiated convention would be cheered by many. Still, a realistic assessment of probabilities suggests that the state legislatures are unlikely to agree on any such process. Many will remain committed to the strategy of trying to persuade the Congress to call the convention, limited to a single amendment or subject. Still others will be convinced that no convention should be called by anyone for any reason.

We have observed before that the political parties do not and will not support an Article V amendatory constitutional convention. They have too much money, time, and effort invested in gaming the system as it exists to step back and consider whether systemic changes in our constitution ought to be considered.

Moreover, the spirit of partisanship runs so deep in the American experience that any discussion of a convention in party circles will immediately devolve into a caucus about using the convention to advance partisan goals and to enhance partisan power.

The founders of our nation, without exception, condemned party politics. George Washington warned against partisanship in his farewell address:

> The alternate domination of one faction over another, sharpened by the spirit of revenge, natural to party dissension, which in different ages and countries has perpetrated the most horrid enormities, is itself a frightful despotism. But this leads at length to a more formal and permanent despotism. The disorders and miseries which result gradually incline the minds of men to seek security and repose in the absolute power of an individual; and sooner or later the chief of some prevailing faction, more able or more fortunate than his competitors,

> turns this disposition to the purposes of his own elevation, on the ruins of public liberty.[1]

I submit that the only practical way for the people of the United States to adopt the kind of systemic constitutional amendments that will address the perceived problems of our federal republic, is for the people themselves to organize and conduct an amendatory constitutional convention. Without the call of Congress. Without concurrent petitions from the state legislatures.

Such a convention would be organized and conducted under the auspices of the 1787 constitution. It would be a true constituent assembly to which nonpartisan delegates from every county in the nation would be chosen by their fellow citizens.

The method and means of doing this are presented in the website at www.conventionusa.org. The apportionment described there divides the nation into districts drawn along county lines in which 6,166 delegates, being one for every 50,000 people, can be chosen. In each district the ratio of delegates to constituents is between one to 45,000 and one to 55,000. The number of delegates allotted to each state is shown in Appendix I.

Whether in a single delegate or a multiple delegate district, voters will be allowed to vote for only one candidate. Voting for a 'slate' will not be accommodated. Not only does this rule comply with the "one man one vote" concept, it also enables minorities to have a voice by uniting behind a favored son or daughter.

As noted earlier, the 50K plan not only assures that delegates are close to the people of their districts, geographically and politically, but it also provides a genuine sampling of American public opinion which is far more reliable than the kind of random polling on which many political decisions are currently being made.

Randomly selected groups as small as 500 people are often cited as identifying the opinion of the mass of the American people on critical issues. Their knowledge base is uneven and their attention to the issue may be and often is very minimal.

Six thousand people selected from geographically and politically distinct areas of the states and given time and opportunity to study and deliberate, will produce a polling result that is not only reliable within a minimal percent, but it will also consist of opinions more knowledgably held and asserted, so as not to be as vulnerable to dissuasion by mass advertising and expensive public relations campaigns.

Unfortunately, it is unrealistically sanguine to expect many state legislatures to adopt the kind of resolution outlined in chapter 2. The Article V issue has been on state legislative agendas for years, and the number of advocates for and against a convention make the resolution of differences daunting to say the least.

Inertia and gridlock are the demons that dance around democracy, and the larger the issue, the smaller are the details wherein the devil is to be found. Still, the national debt increases faster than one million dollars a minute and the sense of urgency among the citizenry grows exponentially.

What are we to do? We, the People. What are our options? Are we compelled, like lambs being led to slaughter, merely to inch our way ever closer to the butcher's block, keeping our composure, keeping our silence, keeping our resignation to the inevitable hatchet as the only solace and comfort within our reach and control?

Or is there something else? Is Big Brother now so big and so ubiquitous that we dare not even whisper the words of the Declaration of Independence? Has our knowledge of statecraft so atrophied that no avenue of protest or reform is left to us but physical confrontation?

THE LAST WORD

Over the past five years, I have made a substantial personal investment of time, effort, and money to organize an Article V convention. It is an endeavor that first captured my interest more than thirty years ago when my law review article was published in 1982. I have done this because I believe that it is a worthy cause; an effort, however novel, however tentative, actually to do something about our dysfunctional government.

I have proceeded on the cautious, conservative premise that what was done by the founders of our nation was wise and fundamentally sound, and that building on the foundation they created is the most prudent and safest way to advance the felicity of our people.

As much as the convening of an amendatory constitutional convention was anticipated and provided for by our forbears, it is nonetheless a bold and controversial idea in the twenty-first century. And doing it without the call of the Congress or the cooperation of the state legislatures must appear impossible if not irrational.

I am asked some very pertinent questions: Will it work? Can 6,166 delegates be found? Who will pay for it? What will it do? Can it accomplish anything? What kind of amendments would it propose? Could any of them be ratified as part of the constitution?

Even more cynically: Is it legal? Is it revolutionary? Can the government forbid it, or break it up? Or finally, even if we did it, would anybody notice? Would anybody care?

I browse the Internet and find Professor Larry Lessig's flashy new website, www.Mayone.us, which announces that over $700,000 has been raised in less than a week. To do what? To fund a new super PAC designed to elect five new Congressmen for the purpose of eliminating the influence of money in politics.

Pardon me? Elect five new Congressmen to do what? "To kick start fundamental reforms by reducing the influence of money in politics." That's what it says. That is what the able, charismatic, and articulate Professor Lessig says they plan to do.

They plan on creating a super PAC to fight the super PACs. They want to raise and spend a lot of money on politics to get people to stop raising and spending a lot of money on politics.

I certainly understand their concern. The unholy alliance of corporate lobbyists and members of Congress is a national disgrace. But I don't think electing five new Congressmen is going to change anything.

In the first place, you can't stop people from spending money on politics by legislation. Money is the mother's milk of politics, because where men are free, money is power.

Politics is simply a civilized substitute for warfare. It's all about power. It is all about who gets to enforce his will at the point of a gun. Trying to limit how much money can be spent on politics is like trying to limit how many speeches a candidate can give, how many hands he can shake or how many hours she can campaign.

The disgraceful torrent of campaign financing in America is the direct result of two factors: the size of the constituencies of elected officials and the amount of legislation that directly affects how much money people receive or keep.

The more the government meddles in the balance sheets of businesses and individuals, either by subsidies, taxes or regulations, the more will be spent trying to influence what government does, and the more a candidate has to spend to communicate with constituents, the more politicians will be beholden to the people who finance campaigns.

There are systemic changes which could be introduced to affect these factors, but five new Congressmen can't bring them about. An Article V amendatory constitutional convention can.

I don't get it. Donating money to a super PAC to kill the super PACs somehow makes sense to people who think that amending the constitution would be a waste of time.

Let me tell you a story. Back in the 1970s, I was a young Chief Justice. Polly and I had six children and no money. I took a part-time job teaching a course on the Constitution at the University of Detroit, ninety miles from our home in East Lansing.

Somehow, I got the bright idea to start a law school in the state capital of Lansing. I thought that, with a few other judges, we might rent an old house, put our personal libraries there, and start tutoring a few students in the evening.

The legal education establishment was aghast. A committee of scholars was appointed by the State Board of Education. They recommended against our charter, insisting that we would have to abide by all of the American Bar Association accreditation standards, and a Michigan statute that required capitalization of $1 million.

About that time, Michigan State University had been trying to get a law school for several years. Every time another legislator got on board, there was a big story in the paper. By contrast, a small article appeared on one of the back pages to the effect that Justice Brennan was starting a law school in Lansing. I got several hundred letters from eager applicants.

I found an exception in the education code that allowed me to equate anticipated income to capital at a rate of 33 to 1. I showed that revenue from our first class would easily exceed that goal. The state board countered with one of their rules requiring that half of the income had to be cash in hand.

I called Bud Stoddard at the Michigan Bank and he gave me a letter of credit for $15,000.

The school opened in rented quarters in January of 1973, with seventy-six students, each of whom had signed an affidavit that he or she knew the school wasn't accredited and they might never get to take a bar exam.

Over the next ten or fifteen years, we fought a continuous battle with the newspapers, the American Bar Association, and the other law schools. Despite the fact that the school was a nonprofit corporation, and I was not being compensated, the press insinuated that I was moonlighting and that somehow there was a conflict of interest between legal education and the administration of justice.

At the end of 1973, I resigned from the Supreme Court to become the full-time dean of the Thomas M. Cooley Law School.

People thought I was crazy. Give up a secure seat on the highest court in the state to run a store-front law school? What was I thinking? It couldn't be done. You can't start a real honest-to-god law school with seventy-six students and a letter of credit.

But we did. And today, the Thomas Cooley Law School is the largest accredited college of law in the United States.

So maybe you can understand what is going through my head. I can see a permanent constitutional convention in America. A convention that operates completely outside of the government. A convention that is supported solely by the voluntary contributions of citizens. A convention that elects delegates every two years concurrent with the congressional elections. A convention that meets in the odd-numbered years and never proposes more than one or two amendments.

It would be a convention populated by ordinary people, interested civic minded Americans, who give their time and talent without compensation to the important task of making sure that the constitution of 1787 remains the bulwark of our freedom and felicity.

It is a vision not readily or easily indulged in by men and women who view politics as a dirty, money-grubbing business, peopled by rascals and crooks, beholden to rich corporate fat cats, bankers and brokers, all of whom are hell bent on squeezing all the liberty out our lives and all the hope out of the American Dream.

I have written this book with the goal that it will somehow convince someone, or some people, with more resources and more time left on this earth than I have, to step up and take hold of the banner of liberty.

The first requisite for leadership is the willingness to grab the brass ring. This is why I have addressed this work to the First Responders across the land. True patriots do not sit at home waiting for the nominating committee to come knocking on the door.

Whether it is election as a city councilman, a school board member, or a member of the legislature, the first person who must believe in a candidacy is the candidate himself or herself.

I cannot accept that there are not 6,166 Americans who are willing to step forward and represent their county at a convention organized to propose necessary amendments to the Constitution of the United States.

I don't mean 6,166 greedy self-serving politicians. I mean 6,166 honorable men and women who are willing to devote time, attention, and energy to the very important work of statecraft involved in identifying and refining amendments that are needed and will be found acceptable by a substantial majority of the citizens of the nation.

Without pay. Without any reward except the knowledge that they have helped in a vitally important and lasting work that will benefit generations yet unborn.

Given the people; given a critical mass of common sense, distributed across the nation in an apportionment scheme that is fair, balanced, and represents the people of the states by a common ratio approximating one to 50,000, there is no law, custom or public policy that can prevent a convention, so constituted, from doing the work our Founders assigned to Article V of the federal charter.

The naysayers will, of course, say nay. Among their first fusillades will be the charge that the delegates are self-selected and have no call to assert that they represent the people of their districts.

The very simple answer to that objection is that the delegates will in fact be elected. Modern technology makes it possible. Candidates for delegate will file on the Internet. Their supporters will vote on the Internet. The system will be simple, straightforward, and tamper-proof.

The official voter registration of candidates and electors will be electronically checked in real time. It is entirely possible that the system will automatically take a "selfie" of the voter, making the process more foolproof than many precincts operating under state election laws.

THE BLANK WALL

A stack of books on my desk evidences the fact that thoughtful Americans have been proposing constitutional amendments for years. Unhappily, the government is like the weather: everybody talks about it, nobody does anything about it. There is an enormous inertia in the land. Whenever amending the constitution is mentioned, people glaze over, shrug their shoulders and change the subject.

Thoughtful men, scholars, and lawyers write about it and offer their suggestions for amendment of the constitution. Breyer, Levin, Lessig, Levinson, Will, Presser, Napolitano, Labunski, Sabato, and Stevens, the list goes on and on. The ideas are novel, clever, revolutionary, and conservative. They are all advanced seriously and invite challenge and debate.

But where are they lodged? Who debates them? Who judges whether they are reasonable, useful, desirable suggestions for amending the federal charter?

The answer is they go no place. They are on no one's agenda. There is no body of jurors charged with the duty of separating the wheat from the chaff. There are no committees waiting to tweak the ideas, contemplate how they would work, consider what would happen if they were adopted and ultimately answer the question whether they would appeal to the broad base of the American electorate.

There is no forum for these constitutional scholars to address, no panel to ask questions, no devil's advocate to poke holes and point out shortcomings. If they are activist enough, the authors can scramble up a camp of followers and launch another website, embark upon another round of visitations to the state capitols seeking to persuade legislators to advance their ideas.

Bill Fruth was a good example. A successful municipal consultant, Fruth decided one day that the constitution should be amended. He wrote a book called *Ten Amendments for Freedom*, had hundreds of copies printed and sent to every state legislator in America. Then he embarked on a tour of state capitols that had him on the road for months.

Nobody blinked. Bill finally teamed up with David Biddulph to form the Balanced Budget Task Force, which has a website, followers, and some money, but no amendment. Presumably, they support other initiatives that might result in a balanced federal budget.

There are others. Kitchen table draftsmen. One that has made the rounds for literally years is called "The Twenty-Eighth Amendment." It presents the colossally impractical idea of requiring that every law that applies to members of Congress must apply to all Americans and vice-versa. Thus every American must have an office in Washington, a staff, and a $175,000 a year salary. And every Congressman must be eligible for food stamps.

Constitutional amendments need to be vetted by a jury of average citizens. People like Amos Singletary and Johnathan Smith, simple farmers—working folks—who can read and understand a constitution which says what it means and means what it says.

Perhaps there are no such people in America today. Perhaps no First Responders will come forward. It wouldn't be the first lost cause that I have embraced. I have failed many times in my long life. I am not afraid of failure.

My children and my students have often heard my mantra for success:

If you drop it, pick it up. If you spill it, wipe it up. If you forget it, go back and get it. If you do it wrong, do it over. If you break it, fix it. If you destroy it, replace it. If you owe it, pay it. If you did it, admit it. And always remember that most of the forward progress we make in the game of life is getting back to the line of scrimmage. Some have even heard my infamous country western song, "Percy Veerance." (He don't quit and he don't cry. Don't shake his fist up at the sky.)

As long as we believe that what we are doing is good and right, that success would be desirable and beneficial to society, we can pursue this enterprise with purpose and vigor. The Internet is there to be used. It is nonpartisan.

The founders of our nation believed that it was possible to weave a fabric of governance by deliberation and debate, consultation, compromise, and consensus. And so they did and so it has been proved.

The recorded history of human civilization demonstrates rather conclusively that governments engaged in continuous warfare and saddled with overwhelming debt are destined to collapse. Typically, they fall either to stronger foreign powers or to civil disorder among the domestic population.

No thinking American can seriously deny that we are traveling down that road; that we have been traveling down that road for more than half a century. Still, the exceptional success of the great American experiment over the last two centuries has prompted most Americans to believe that sort of thing can't happen here. Unfortunately, being in Utopia and being in Denial feel pretty much the same.

There are twenty-six counties in the United States called "Franklin" and twenty-six more named "Jefferson." There are twenty-four Lincolns and twenty-four Jacksons. The most popular county name is Washington. There are thirty-one counties named for the First President.

You can't scroll down through the counties in America without being impressed that at the local level, at the community level, the American people treasure and honor their political roots.

The Founders knew that true democracy is a local phenomenon. The town hall was always the womb of liberty. We continue to pay tribute to the grassroots as the true source of political power. Americans revolt at being treated like statistics. People are not mere numbers, to be polled and manipulated. They need representatives who look and sound and feel as they do. People from their neighborhood, from their town, from their county.

What we have done on these pages may not be the best and final answer. I submit, however, that it is faithful to the vision of the Founders, and that should recommend it.

Adlai Stevenson once described apathetic Americans as those whose motto was "Don't just do something . . . stand there." Perhaps that also describes what Richard Nixon called, "The Silent Majority."

I have known too many volunteers and risk takers in my eighty-four years to believe that there are not enough First Responders to save the nation. In January of 1973, when I welcomed seventy-six men and women to the inaugural class of the Thomas Cooley Law School, I told them it was a moment to taste and feel the creativity of the human spirit.

Our faith in ourselves and in each other, our belief that what we were doing together would someday benefit men and women as yet unborn was as real as the light bulbs over our heads and the sound of our voices. Some day, I said, the school would be known for its buildings, its library, its faculty and alumni. And when that day came, it would seem that Cooley Law School always was, that it was somehow the legacy of a nineteenth century jurist.

In the same way, an Article V convention is, after all, nothing more nor less than a human endeavor, an idea, a dream, a people-thing, created out of the imagination and determination of men and women who believe in it and are willing to share the burden and make it happen.

The Creator endowed us with inalienable rights. He also endowed us with indomitable spirit. The Constitution is ours. We mean to keep it.

NOTES

1. George Washington, Farewell Address.

Appendix

This list shows the number of delegates and districts in each State and the ratio of constituents to delegates.

State	*Population*	*Delegates*	*Districts*	*Ratio*
Alabama	4,779,649	96	26	50,603
Alaska	710,231	14	3	47,471
Arizona	6,392,017	128	10	50,248
Arkansas	2,915,917	58	26	50,352
California	37,253,956	745	35	50,788
Colorado	5,029,196	101	21	50,601
Connecticut	3,574,097	71	6	50,243
Delaware	897,934	18	3	50,781
Florida	18,801,310	376	40	50,362
Georgia	9,687,653	194	55	50,978
Hawaii	1,360,301	27	3	50,565
Idaho	1,567,582	31	16	51,730
Illinois	12,830,632	257	34	50,031
Indiana	6,483,802	130	32	51,006
Iowa	3,046,355	61	22	50,637
Kansas	2,853,118	57	21	51,071

State	*Population*	*Delegates*	*Districts*	*Ratio*
Kentucky	4,339,367	87	28	49,183
Louisiana	4,533,372	91	26	50,383
Maine	1,328,361	27	7	49,911
Maryland	5,773,552	115	12	50,133
Massachusetts	6,547,629	131	11	50,107
Michigan	9,883,640	198	38	50,293
Minnesota	5,303,925	106	25	51,387
Mississippi	2,967,297	59	25	50,523
Missouri	5,988,927	120	79	50,725
Montana	989,415	20	8	50,379
Nebraska	1,826,341	37	16	48,889
Nevada	2,700,551	54	7	48,836
New Hampshire	1,316,470	26	4	48,993
New Jersey	8,791,894	176	19	50,044
New Mexico	2,059,179	388	32	50,847
New York	19,378,102	41	12	48,934
North Carolina	9,535,483	191	44	49,904
North Dakota	672,591	14	7	48,417
Ohio	11,536,504	231	43	49,649
Oklahoma	3,751,351	75	28	50,054
Oregon	3,831,074	77	17	49,360
Pennsylvania	12,702,379	254	39	50,338
Rhode Island	1,052,567	21	3	52,231
South Carolina	4,625,364	93	23	50,000
South Dakota	814,180	16	9	51,416
Tennessee	6,346,105	127	36	50,212
Texas	25,145,561	503	58	50,321
Utah	2,763,885	55	12	49,936
Vermont	625,741	13	16	48,625
Virginia	8,001,024	160	92	50,409
Washington	6,724,540	134	18	50,399

State	*Population*	*Delegates*	*Districts*	*Ratio*
West Virginia	1,852,994	37	40	49,548
Wisconsin	5,686,986	114	33	49,654
Wyoming	563,626	11	8	51,890
TOTAL	308,143,728	6,166		

Bibliography

Bleyer, Kevin. *Me The People: One Man's Selfless Quest to Rewrite the Constitution of the United States*. New York: Random House, 2012.

Bowen, Catherine Drinker. *Miracle at Philadelphia*. New York: Little Brown, 1966.

Buckley, F. H. *The Once and Future King: The Rise of Crown Government in America, .* New York: Encounter Books, 2014.

de Tocqueville, Alexis. *Democracy in America* . New York: Random House, 1945.

Ervin, Sam J. and Clark, Ramsey. *Role of the Supreme Court: Policymaker or Adjudicator?*. Washington, DC: American Enterprise Institute, 1970.

Guerra, Darren Patrick. *Perfecting The Constitution: The Case for the Article V Amendment Process.* Lanham, MD: Lexington Books, 2013.

Kyvig, David E.. *Explicit and Authentic Acts: Amending the U.S. Constitution 1776-1995.* Lawrence: University Press of Kansas, 1996.

Labunski, Richard E. *The Second Constitutional Convention: How The American People Can Take Back Their Government.* Versailles, KY: Marley and Beck Press, 2000.

Lessig, Lawerence, *Republic, Lost: How Money Corrupts Congress—and a Plan to Stop It.* New York: Hachette, 2011.

Levin, Mark R. *The Liberty Amendments: Restoring the American Republic.* New York: Threshold Editions, 2013.

Levinson, Sanford. *Our Undemocratic Constitution: Where the Constitution Has Gone Wrong (And How We The People Can Correct It).* New York: Oxford University Press, 2006.

Mason, Alpheus Thomas and William M. Beaney. *The Supreme Court in a Free Society.* New York: W.W. Norton and Company, 1968.

McClanahan, Brion. *The Founding Fathers Guide to the Constitution/* Washington, DC: Regnery Publishing, 2012.

Napolitano, Andrew P. *Constitutional Chaos: What Happens When The Government Breaks Its Own Laws.* Nashville, TN: Thomas Nelson, Inc. 2004.

Presser, Stephen B. *Recapturing the Constitution: Race, Religion, and Abortion Reconsidered.* Washington, DC: Regnery Publishing, 1994)

Sabato, Larry J. *A More Perfect Constitution: 25 Proposals to Revitalize Our Constitution and Make America a Fairer Country.* New York: Walker Publishing Company, 2007.

Will, George F. *Restoration: Congress, Term Limits and the Recovery of Deliberative Democracy.* New York, The Free Press, 1992.

Woods Jr., Thomas E. and Gutzman, Kevin R. *Who Killed The Constitution? The Federal Government vs American Liberty from World War I to Barack Obama.* New York, Three Rivers Press, 2008.

Index

About the Author

A graduate of the University of Detroit Law School, Thomas E. Brennan was elected Judge of the Common Pleas Court of Detroit in 1961, after losing five elections, including one for a seat in the U.S. House of Representatives. Appointed to the Wayne County Circuit Court by Governor George Romney in 1963, Brennan was elected to a full six year term in 1964. In 1966, he was elected to the Michigan Supreme Court, where he was chosen by his colleagues to serve as Chief Justice in 1969 and 1970. In 1972, he founded the Thomas M. Cooley Law School in Lansing, Michigan, and on January 1, 1974, he resigned from the bench to become the first Dean of Cooley Law School. He remained at the school in various capacities until 2002, overseeing the accreditation and growth of the school to become the largest college of law in the United States. In addition to his many judicial opinions and law review articles, Judge Brennan wrote a novel about judicial intrigue entitled *The Bench* (2000). Brennan is the founder of Convention USA, a citizens initiative to promote an Article V convention.

Lightning Source UK Ltd.
Milton Keynes UK
UKOW04n0322161217
314508UK00011B/725/P

9 781498 501033